Launchpad

Taking The Leap

Author: Andrea Pluck

Cover page by Jeremy Pluck

Cover Art: "Leap of Liberty", by Andrew Baines

First published in 2025 in Australia by
Pluck Pluck Goose Publishing
1 Vaucluse Crescent
Bellevue Heights, South Australia
5050

PPG
PLUCK PLUCK GOOSE PUBLISHING

ISBN 978-0-9756253-8-5

9 780975 625385

Acknowledgements

This book was written with the encouragement, talents, and generosity of the people around me.

To my husband Jeremy—thank you for bringing your design skills, sharp eyes, and calm editing energy to this project (and to so many others). You keep believing in me even when at times I struggle to believe in myself. You keep telling me I could do this myself, but honestly, we both know I rely heavily on your input.

To my friend and talented artist Andrew Baines—thank you for generously allowing me to feature your painting on the cover. Your work brings beauty, depth, and feeling to this book before a single page is turned. I am honoured to share it here.

To my friends, colleagues, and students—your stories, questions, and lived experiences have shaped this book in ways you may not realise. Every conversation, every workshop, every moment of "Oh, I wish someone had told me that..." helped build these pages.

And finally, to every massage therapist who is just beginning—thank you for the work you are about to step into. It matters. You matter. This book is for you.

About the Author

Hi, I'm Andrea—massage therapist, educator, writer, and someone who vividly remembers what it feels like to graduate with equal parts of excitement and "what on earth do I do now?"

When I first entered the massage profession, I had passion, a newish but solid skillset, and a head full of questions. The leap from student clinic to real-world practice felt bigger than expected—and no one was talking about the emotional, logistical, and financial realities of getting started. So, I learned the long way: through trial, error, honest conversations, and a lot of figuring things out as I went.

For more than a decade now, I've worked in clinics, partnered with health professionals, set up my own practice, taught new therapists, and created training programs for others making this leap. What I've come to believe is this: being a skilled therapist is only part of the puzzle. Building a sustainable, ethical, and joyful career takes support, strategy, and self-awareness.

I wrote this book to be the kind of guide I wish I'd had—something grounded and realistic, but also encouraging and empowering. Whether you're starting your own business, joining a team, or still figuring out your next step, I hope this book helps you feel a little more equipped, a little more confident, and a lot less alone.

You don't have to be perfect. You don't have to have it all figured out. You just have to start. Be open, have courage and a willingness to grow.

Disclaimer

The content in this book is based on my firsthand experiences, professional knowledge, and research. It is intended for educational and informational purposes only and should not be considered medical, legal, or financial advice. While I strive to provide accurate and up-to-date information, I make no guarantees regarding the completeness, reliability, or applicability of the content to individual circumstances.

By engaging with this material, you acknowledge that I am not responsible for any outcomes—positive or negative—that may result from applying the concepts discussed. Your success depends on your unique situation, actions, and professional judgment.

Some names in this book have been changed to protect the privacy of individuals. Some have been changed simply because it felt right.

If you have any concerns or require specific advice, please seek guidance from an appropriate expert.

Introduction

Why This Book Exists

Starting your massage career is exciting—but let's be honest, it can also be overwhelming. You finish your studies, step out into the real world, and suddenly you're faced with decisions you didn't even know you'd need to make: Where should I work? How do I set my prices? Should I go solo or work for someone else? What if I mess something up?

This book is here to walk beside you through all of that.

Think of *Launchpad* as your friendly, no-fluff companion for the first phase of your professional journey. I won't promise overnight success. But I *will* share what I've learned from years in this field—both the wins and the stumbles—and offer you practical guidance, thoughtful questions, and a whole lot of reassurance along the way.

Whether you're planning to open your own space, rent a room in an existing clinic, or step into a busy workplace as a contractor or employee, this book will help you do it with more clarity, confidence, and care.

This is about more than just starting a business. It's about building a career that aligns with who you are, how you want to work, and the kind of therapist you're becoming.

You don't need to have all the answers right now. You just need a place to begin. Let's start here—together.

How to Use This Book

This book is designed to be both a guide and a resource. You can read it from start to finish, or dip into the chapters that feel most relevant to you right now.

Each section is packed with practical tools, real-world examples, and personal reflections. I've also put in some reflection prompts and checklists to help you apply the ideas to your own life and business, so feel free to highlight, scribble in the margins, or revisit them later.

To support your learning beyond this book, you'll also find suggestions for further reading, as well as links to related online courses or templates you can access separately.

Most of all, this book is meant to feel like a place to pause, think, and make plans you can follow through on.

There's no one-size-fits-all approach to building a massage career—but there *are* thoughtful, flexible paths forward. You're here. You're ready. Let's find yours.

Contents

Part One:
Laying the Groundwork

Chapter 1: Not Just a Job

Starting strong, even when you feel unsure.

Congratulations! You've finished your course. You've learned the muscles, passed your exams, practiced your techniques, and maybe even survived your first real massage in the wild. And now you're standing at the edge of something big: a career. A profession. A business. A calling.

It's exciting. It's a little scary. And if you're anything like I was at the start, it's also full of questions you didn't expect to be asking.

"Where do I start?"

"Where should I work?"

"Am I really ready?"

"What if I mess up?"

"Can I actually make a living doing this?"

Let's begin right here: *You're not alone in wondering.* And no, you don't have to have it all figured out to take your next step.

This Work Is More Than Technique

Massage therapy is not just about hands-on skills. It's about connection. It's about presence. It's about being a calm, thoughtful presence in someone's day—often during a time when they're dealing with pain, stress, or emotional overwhelm. The technical stuff matters, of course. But what people remember most? It's how they felt with you.

It took me a while to learn that. In the beginning, I worried constantly about doing it "right." Was my pressure OK? Did I miss a spot? Was I professional enough, warm enough, confident enough? But slowly, with each client, I realised that the work we do is also deeply human. It's relational. And if you care—if you show up with attention and integrity—you're already doing something valuable.

The Transition Is Real

Graduating from massage school is a strange kind of milestone. You've just finished something big, but the real learning is about to begin. And here's the part they don't always tell you: transitioning from student to professional isn't automatic. It's a shift in mindset, identity, and responsibility. Suddenly, you're not just *practicing* on clients—you're *caring* for them. You're making business decisions. You're setting boundaries. You're figuring out what kind of therapist you want to be.

You might be setting up your own practice. Or maybe you're stepping into a clinic, unsure of how you'll fit in. You might even be juggling massage with another job while you build slowly. Whichever way you begin, there is no one "right" way to launch your career. There is only the way that works for you, in your life, with your values and goals at the centre.

You Are Allowed to Learn as You Go

One of the biggest myths we absorb—especially in health professions—is that we're supposed to know everything right away. But the truth is, most of us are learning in layers. Each client teaches you something. Each decision shapes you. Each misstep helps you grow a little more solid.

When I stepped into massage therapy, I was walking away from a job most people thought was ideal. I had a full-time salary but only worked part-time hours. On paper, it was a dream setup. But something in me was restless. I wanted more meaning, more purpose, more connection in my work. Still, leaving that security behind was terrifying. I remember second-guessing myself constantly in those early days, especially when I was sick for a few weeks and suddenly had no income. Was I being foolish? Was I chasing something unrealistic?

But every time I held space for a client, every time I saw someone breathe easier or move more freely, I knew I was doing the right thing. I wasn't just building a new job—I was building a different life. And even though I didn't have all the answers, I kept going. *You don't have to know everything to begin*. You just have to keep moving, one thoughtful step at a time.

I wrote this book because I wanted you to have a guide. Not a rulebook, not a shortcut—but a thoughtful, realistic, and hopefully reassuring companion through the beginning of your career. I'll share what I've learned from building a practice, mentoring therapists, and navigating the ups and downs of this profession.

This is about more than starting a business. It's about stepping into your role as a professional—and learning how to do that without losing your heart in the process.

What to Expect from This Book

Each chapter is practical, readable, and full of real-world tools and stories, checklists, reflection prompts for you, and ideas you can use right away. You'll learn about business structure, pricing, marketing, ethics, communication, client care, and sustainability. And you'll be reminded that your wellbeing matters as much as your success.

This is your *launchpad*—a place to take off from, not to be perfect in.

So, take a deep breath. You don't have to know it all. You just have to begin.

You've already taken the first step.

Your Personal Launchpad

Take a few quiet minutes—grab a notebook, make a cuppa, and find a space where you can think clearly.

These questions aren't a test. They're a starting point. Be honest. Be kind to yourself. There's no "right" answer—just *your* answer.

- Where am I right now in my massage journey?

- What stage am I at—emotionally, logistically, and professionally?
- What excites me most about starting my career?
- What am I looking forward to? What lights me up?
- What scares me or makes me hesitate?
- Are there specific worries I have about this transition?
- What does "success" mean to me in this profession?
- Is it about freedom, Impact, Financial stability, Work-life balance?
- What kind of therapist do I want to become?
- Think beyond technique—what kind of space do I want to hold for others? What kind of energy do I want to bring to my work?
- What do I need to remind myself when self-doubt creeps in?

Write a sentence or mantra you can come back to when the wobbles happen.

I found this helpful when I first started. It's something you can come back to time and again. Your answers will change. Sometimes it's just nice to look back and see how far you've come.

Chapter 2: Making the Shift – From Student to Professional

From Student to Professional. It's more than a certificate.

There's something magical (and slightly terrifying) about finishing massage school. You've a couple of years studying, practicing, being supervised, and ticking off assessments. And then, just like that, the safety net disappears. No more clinic supervisors to debrief with. No more class schedules. No more pass/fail boxes. It's just you, your skills, and your next steps.

This chapter is all about helping you navigate that shift—not just practically, but emotionally and professionally.

Because here's the truth: being qualified doesn't automatically mean feeling ready.

Leaving the Nest: Why This Transition Feels Big

When you're in student clinic, you're held. There's a roster. Someone else does the advertising. The clients expect you to be learning. You have supervisors to double-check things with, and everything happens in a clearly defined structure.

Then suddenly, the scaffolding falls away.

You might find yourself thinking:

- "Can I do this on my own?"

- "What if a client asks me something I don't know?"

- "What happens if I make a mistake?"

These thoughts are normal. Every therapist—every single one—goes through this shift. What matters isn't being fearless. It's recognising that fear and building confidence anyway.

Internal Shift: Claiming the Role

Part of the transition from student to professional is an internal one. It's not just about what you do—it's about how you see yourself.

There's a moment when you stop saying "I'm studying massage" and start saying, "I'm a massage therapist." And for many of us, that moment doesn't come as quickly as the certificate in our hands.

If that's you, don't worry. These adjustments to change take time. Confidence builds through doing. Each client you support, each appointment you complete, each decision you make on your own—all of it reinforces the reality that you *are* a professional. You're not faking it. You're growing into it.

Real talk

I remember finishing my final student clinic and walking out into the sunlight, feeling more daunted than proud. I had my diploma, yes—but I also had a severe case of imposter syndrome. It wasn't until I started seeing real clients, solving real problems, and having real conversations that something inside me started to settle. It took a little while. The doing made it real.

External Shift: Professional Presentation

As a student, your environment did a lot of the presenting for you. Now, you're in charge of how you show up.

Professionalism doesn't mean being stiff or robotic. It's about showing care, clarity, and consistency. That means:

- Being on time.
- Having systems in place.

- Communicating clearly.

- Taking responsibility for outcomes.

- Dressing and behaving in a way that reflects the kind of service you offer.

It doesn't have to be perfect. You're allowed to learn as you go. But your clients will notice whether you take yourself, and your role seriously.

Boundaries and Decision-Making

This transition is also about taking ownership of your choices. You'll need to decide:

- What kind of work you want to do.

- What kind of clients you want to see.

- Where you'll work.

- What your policies are.

- What happens when something goes wrong.

These aren't easy decisions—but they are empowering ones. And unlike in student life, no one is going to give you the "right" answer. You get to craft the version of this career that fits your values, energy, and goals.

This book will help you with those decisions, one by one.

You Don't Need to Know Everything

Let me say this as clearly as possible: no one expects you to be an expert from day one (except, perhaps yourself). Your clients aren't looking for perfection—they're looking for someone they trust, someone who listens, and someone who holds space with skill and care.

So, give yourself permission to grow. To ask questions. To keep learning. You'll get more comfortable over time. And you'll look back in a year or two and be amazed at how far you've come.

Therapist Story: Sarah's First Solo Client

Sarah had just graduated and was renting a small room in a local wellness centre. She'd spent weeks getting everything ready—choosing towels, printing forms, creating a logo she wasn't sure about. She had a booking system, a price list, even a Spotify playlist of calming instrumental tracks (and a license from OneMusic Australia to do so).

But when her first paying client walked through the door—a real, full-fee client, not a student clinic volunteer—her stomach flipped.

"I suddenly forgot everything I'd learned," she told me later. "I couldn't remember the intake script I'd practiced. My hands felt awkward. I was so nervous I nearly forgot to ask if they had any allergies."

But here's what happened next: Sarah breathed. She smiled. She connected. She listened.

And when the client left, they said, "That was exactly what I needed. Thank you."

Sarah cried in her car afterward. Not because it was perfect. But because she'd done it.

"It wasn't about being flawless," she said. "It was about showing up—and starting."

My First Snoozing Client

In one of my very first professional sessions, a client fell asleep on the table—and I completely froze.

No one had ever told me what to do if someone nodded off. Should I keep going? Should I check if they were okay? Should I quietly sneak out of the room and pretend I'd never been there?

I remember standing there, mid-stroke, completely unsure of what the "right" move was. Eventually, I just kept massaging. They woke up at the end and told me it was the most relaxed they'd felt in months.

That day taught me two things. First: if a client falls asleep, it's usually a compliment. Second: there will always be situations you weren't explicitly trained for—but you *can* handle them with care and common sense.

Reflect: Growing into the Role

These questions will help you check in with yourself as you cross this threshold from student to professional.

What are the biggest differences I've noticed between being a student and stepping into professional life?

How does it feel in my body? What's changed in how others relate to me?

In what ways do I still feel like a student? In what ways do I already feel like a professional?

It's okay to be in between.

What qualities do I want to bring to my professional identity?

Think of the kind of therapist you want to be—warm, thoughtful, grounded, confident, curious?

What stories am I telling myself about being "ready"?

Are those stories true? Helpful? Or ready to be rewritten?

What support systems can I put in place to help me through this transition?

Supervision, peer support, regular check-ins, or ongoing education?

Chapter 3: Cultivating a Business Mindset

Thinking like a practitioner—and a professional.

When we picture becoming a massage therapist, we often imagine the hands-on work: the calm rooms, the meaningful connections, the difference we can make. What we don't always picture is the spreadsheet, the tax file number, or the moment someone asks, "What do you charge?"—and we realise we're not entirely sure.

But here's the truth: if you plan to work for yourself in any capacity—or even just want to build a steady, sustainable career—you *are* in business. That doesn't mean you need to become a cut-throat entrepreneur. It just means you're in the driver's seat. And that takes a different kind of mindset.

From Helper to Professional

Massage therapists often come into this work because we care. We want to help. We want to make people feel better. That's beautiful—and important. But caring alone won't pay the rent or manage your schedule. If we want to keep helping people for the long haul, we need to treat our work as valuable. And that means treating it like a business.

This can feel uncomfortable at first. You might feel awkward about charging money, or unsure about "selling" yourself. But having a business mindset isn't about being pushy—it's about being clear, confident, and prepared. It's about giving your practice the structure it needs to support *you*, not just your clients.

Shifting Gears: Thinking Like a Business Owner

So, what does a business mindset look like? Here are a few key shifts that will serve you well:

- **From just doing the work** to also thinking about how the work fits into your life, goals, and income.

- **From waiting for clients to find you** to planning how to reach the people you can best serve.

- **From hoping for success** to creating systems and habits that support it.

A business mindset means understanding that your time, energy, and skills are finite—and worth protecting. It means making choices based on sustainability, not just survival.

When I first started, I said yes to everything. Every client, every time slot, every opportunity—just to keep busy. It took me a while to realise I was burning out and undercharging. Developing a business mindset helped me become more intentional. I started asking: *Is this working for me?* And if it wasn't—I changed it.

Permission to be New at This

You don't need to know everything about business to begin. But you do need to stay open, curious, and willing to learn. You might make some awkward pricing decisions. You might underestimate your time or forget to track something. That's OK. Business is a skill, just like massage—and you get better at it with practice.

You're not expected to be perfect. But you *are* allowed to take yourself seriously.

Aligning Values and Vision

One of the most empowering parts of cultivating a business mindset is that you get to shape your work around your values. You get to decide:

- What kind of clients you want to serve.

- What kind of space you want to create.

- How you want to show up in the world.

This isn't about copying someone else's success. It's about defining what *success* means to you—and then building a practice that supports that.

Shaping Your Mindset

This journaling activity is here to help you clarify how you want to show up professionally—both practically and personally.

How do I currently feel about calling myself a business owner? (Is it exciting? Intimidating? Something I hadn't even thought about?)

What are my biggest worries when it comes to business and money? (Write them down without judgement.)

What does a successful massage career look like to me? (Think beyond income. What kind of rhythm do you want your life and work to have?)

What boundaries do I already know I need to protect my time, energy, and values? (Are you someone who tends to over give? Say yes too quickly?)

What's one small step I can take this week to support my mindset as a professional? (Maybe it's tracking your time. Maybe it's setting a new boundary. Maybe it's just saying aloud, "I run a business.")

"How Much Should I Charge?"

This is one of the first questions new therapists ask—and for good reason. Pricing feels personal. It ties into our self-worth, our confidence, and our comfort with talking about money. And it's often wrapped in worry: *What if I charge too much? What if no one books? What if I'm not "experienced enough"?*

Here's the short answer:

Charge a rate that reflects your time, skill, and expenses—and allows your business to be sustainable. You didn't go through all that study and training just to scrape by.

But there's no one-size-fits-all price. It depends on where you live, your overheads, your experience, and your goals. And yes, we'll unpack all of that in more detail in a later chapter, including how to set prices with confidence *and* communicate them clearly.

For now, just know this:

Charging fairly doesn't make you greedy. It makes your work sustainable.

And a sustainable practice is one that can help more people, for longer. A lot of new therapists under-change. A lot. We will cover pricing in a later chapter.

Chapter 4: Responsibility and Autonomy

You're the grown-up now (but you don't have to do it alone).

When you're a student, someone else holds the frame. There's a timetable. There are supervisors. There's a clinical structure to lean on. You're given direction and feedback, and decisions are shared. But once you step into professional practice—whether that's in a clinic, your own space, or someone else's—things start to shift.

You become the one setting the tone. You're the one clients turn to for answers. You're the one managing your time, your boundaries, your income, your energy.

Welcome to the world of **professional autonomy**.

It's empowering. It's freeing. It's also... a little overwhelming at times.

Let's unpack what this really means.

You Are Now the Adult in the Room

Autonomy doesn't just mean working solo. It means taking ownership of your choices, your outcomes, and your professional presence. It's recognising that *you* are now responsible for:

- Showing up on time and prepared.

- Managing your bookings and follow-ups.

- Navigating ethical decisions in real time.

- Responding professionally to client needs, boundaries, and feedback.

- Maintaining your own learning and development.

This isn't about perfection—it's about maturity. It's about knowing that clients will sometimes look to you for leadership, and being ready to meet them there, calmly, and competently.

The Freedom Can Be a Shock

Let's be honest—suddenly being *in charge* of yourself can feel like being let loose without a map. There is no supervisor to double-check with. No one reminding you when to renew your insurance or how to handle a late cancellation. You might be surprised by how much of your day is spent managing things that are not strictly "massage."

But this is also where the beauty lies.

You get to decide:

- What kind of therapist you want to be.

- What your workdays look like.

- Who you work with.

- What your policies are.

- How you respond to challenges.

There is a power in that kind of self-trust. And like any power, it grows with practice.

Real Responsibility Isn't About Guilt—It's About Being Grounded

Sometimes, responsibility gets mistaken for pressure. But being responsible doesn't mean taking on everything, burning out, or saying yes to what you can't manage. It means acting with care. It means knowing your limits. It means owning your mistakes and learning from them.

Professional responsibility includes:

- Keeping accurate and secure records.

- Communicating clearly and respectfully.

- Following your scope of practice.

- Seeking support or supervision when you are unsure.

- Taking accountability without shame.

Autonomy Does not Mean Isolation

You can be autonomous *and* supported. You don't have to do this alone. In fact, having a professional network, mentors, or peer support can help you hold your autonomy more confidently. It means you have people to check in with, share challenges with, and keep learning alongside.

When I first started, I felt like I had to prove I could do everything alone. But over time, I realised that real professionalism isn't about isolation—it's about knowing when to reach out. I joined a peer group, found a mentor, and even now, years later, I still value those quiet conversations where I can ask, "What would you do in this situation?"

Your Choices Shape Your Practice

Here is the part that feels scary but is also deeply empowering: your practice will evolve in the direction of your choices. That means:

- If you let boundaries slide, they'll keep sliding.

- If you're deliberate and consistent, clients will feel that clarity.

- If you adjust as you go, your work will keep becoming more aligned with who you are.

Autonomy isn't just about calling the shots—it's about being thoughtful with your choices.

Therapist Story: Lena and the No-Show

Lena had just started working from her home clinic. She had printed off intake forms, set up calming playlists, and even baked muffins for her first week of clients. Things were going smoothly—until a new client booked a 90-minute session... and didn't show up.

"I sat there watching the clock," Lena told me later. "I'd prepared the room, cleared my afternoon, and then... nothing. No message, no apology. I didn't know whether to be worried or annoyed. Honestly, I felt both."

In student clinic, no-shows were rare—and usually managed by staff. But now, Lena was the one who had to respond.

She took a deep breath, sent a gentle check-in message, and then sat down to write her first cancellation policy. "I realised I didn't actually have one yet," she laughed. "That session was unpaid, but it taught me a lot. I needed boundaries—not just for my clients, but for myself."

Lena posted her new cancellation policy the next day. And yes, her next client showed up on time—and loved the session.

"That experience didn't feel great in the moment," she said. "But it made me feel more like a professional. I got to decide how I wanted to be treated—and that made all the difference."

Stepping Into Autonomy

Let's take a quiet moment to check in with how you're feeling about autonomy and responsibility in this new phase of your career.

- What parts of autonomy feel exciting or freeing to me?
- Where am I looking forward to having more control?
- What parts feel uncertain or challenging?

- Be honest—are there things I'd rather someone else still managed?
- What support structures do I need to hold my autonomy with more confidence?
- Think: supervision, systems, community, admin help, resources?
- How do I want to define "professional responsibility" for myself?
- What does it look like in action, not just in theory?
- What's one small way I can practice grounded autonomy this week?

Chapter 5: Self-Care in a Solo Practice

Caring for others starts with caring for yourself.

When you run your own practice whether it's from home, a clinic, or a rented room, it's easy to feel like you must be everything at once: therapist, admin assistant, marketing manager, laundry person, bookkeeper, and cleaner.

And while that kind of independence can be empowering, it also comes with a hidden risk: neglecting your own care while caring for everyone else.

Let's talk about how to build a practice that doesn't just look good on paper—but also *feels* good.

You Are the Business—and the Human Behind It

One of the biggest mindset shifts you'll make is understanding that your energy, health, and clarity are as essential to your practice as your table or oils.

You *are* the business. If you're depleted, the whole thing feels shaky. And in a solo role, there isn't someone to tag in when you're tired, unwell, or overwhelmed.

So, self-care isn't a luxury. It's not something you get to after everything else. It's the scaffolding that holds your business up.

Signs You're Neglecting Your Own Needs

In solo practice, it can sneak up on you—especially when you love your work. But here are some signs your own care might be falling by the wayside:

- You're eating lunch standing up between clients (or skipping it entirely).

- You keep working late to catch up on admin or laundry.

- You haven't taken a proper break in months.

- You're starting to dread client days or feel resentful.

- You find yourself pushing through fatigue instead of pausing.

If any of these feel familiar, you're not failing—you're just running on empty. And it's time to refill the tank.

What Self-Care *Really* Looks Like in Practice

Forget the bubble baths and face masks (unless those are your thing). Self-care, when you're running a solo massage practice, often looks very practical—and sometimes even boring.

It starts with booking regular time off, even if you're not going away. You don't need a holiday planned to deserve a break. Just a breather, a pause, a reset. That space is crucial for your nervous system and creativity.

It also means setting realistic client loads—and sticking to them. Just because you *can* squeeze in another client doesn't mean you *should*. Your energy is limited.

Self-care also shows up in the boundaries you hold around communication. That might mean turning off message notifications after hours or only replying to bookings during work hours. It's okay to have clear limits—and to communicate them with kindness.

Creating simple rituals can help you transition in and out of work mode. This might be a few minutes of deep breathing before your first client, a quick tidy of the room between sessions, or changing your clothes at the end of the day to symbolically "leave work."

Investing in your physical comfort is another form of self-care. Good shoes, supportive flooring, ergonomic tools, and nourishing meals may seem small—but they'll carry you further than hustle and grit ever will.

And of course, keeping your day sustainable is key. That includes building in gaps between clients, having days without bookings, and resisting the pressure to work nonstop. You're building a career, not running a sprint.

You Don't Need to Earn Your Rest

Many of us were raised with the idea that rest is something we get *after* we've worked hard enough. But when you run your own practice, that thinking can backfire fast. There's *always* more to do. For example: emails, towels, bookings, marketing.

Rest doesn't come when the to-do list is finished. It comes when you prioritise it like you do any other appointment.

Give yourself permission to take breaks without guilt. To close your books for a week if you need to. To have days when you don't think about massage at all. You're a human, not a machine.

Community is a Kind of Self-Care

Working solo doesn't have to mean feeling isolated. In fact, one of the kindest things you can do for yourself is to stay connected with other therapists.

Joining a peer support group or a professional association can make a dramatic difference—not just for your learning, but for your sense of belonging. Even informal connections like catching up for coffee with a fellow therapist or sharing ideas in a group chat can help you feel less alone in the work.

You might also consider working with a mentor or supervisor— someone you can check in with, ask questions, and talk things through when the emotional weight of the job starts to build up.

You don't have to figure everything out by yourself. And honestly? It's more sustainable—and more enjoyable—when you don't.

Designing Your Care

Let's take some time to check in with how you're supporting *yourself* in your work.

How do I currently care for myself in my practice? (Think about the small things: breaks, meals, movement, boundaries.)

What areas are feeling depleted or unsustainable? (What do you keep telling yourself you'll "get to eventually"?)

What habits or rituals help me feel grounded and well? (Morning routines, music, time outdoors, journaling, supervision?)

What kind of support—emotional, practical, or professional—do I need more of? (And what might help me build that support into my life?)

If my business were built around caring for me *as well as* my clients, what would that look like?

Therapist Story: A Burnout Wake-Up Call

Nina had always given 110%. She loved her work, her clients, and the feeling of being helpful. In her first year of solo practice, she poured herself into it. She was determined to make it a success, saying yes to every client, replying to messages late at night, and squeezing in "just one more" session—even when her body begged for rest.

At first, it felt great. Her books were filling. She was getting word-of-mouth referrals. People loved her. But slowly, cracks started to show.

"I'd wake up and feel already tired," Nina said. "My hands hurt, my mood was flat, and I started dreading the sound of a booking notification. That was the scariest part—realising that something I loved was making me feel awful."

One day, after a long stretch of back-to-back clients and skipped lunches, she hit a wall. She forgot a returning client's name. Not just a momentary blank—she couldn't remember anything about them until halfway through the session. "I felt so unprofessional. I cried after they left."

That moment became her wake-up call. Nina took the next day off. She turned her phone off and went for a long walk. Then she sat down and asked herself: *What do I need, so I can keep doing this work without losing myself?*

From that point on, she made some changes. She capped the number of clients she saw each week. She blocked out a proper lunch break. She added one admin day per fortnight—and took a real holiday, something she hadn't done in years.

"I had to unlearn the idea that more clients meant more success," Nina said. "Now, success means I can do great work *and* feel good in my life."

Takeaway Thought

"You can't pour from an empty cup—but you *can* build a practice that keeps your cup full."

Your wellbeing isn't something extra you deal with on the side. It's right at the centre of your business—it affects everything. The better you care for yourself, the more sustainable your work becomes. Self-care isn't selfish. It's a skill, a strategy, and a kindness that ripples out to every client you serve.

Take the time to build the kind of practice that supports *you*, not just your bookings.

Chapter 6: Working in a Team or Clinic Setting

Thriving in shared spaces and learning from others.

Not everyone launches into massage by setting up their own practice. In fact, many therapists begin by working within an established team—whether that's a multi-practitioner clinic, a wellness centre, a physio practice, or even a spa environment. And that can be an incredibly valuable way to gain experience, confidence, and community.

But working in a shared space is different from being a student on a roster. You're no longer being supervised—you're a peer. You're no longer in training—you're a professional. Let's talk about how to step into a team with professionalism, presence, and healthy expectations.

Shared Space, Shared Values

The best clinic environments are built on shared respect and aligned values. You don't all have to work the same way—but it helps if the overall culture supports your approach to care.

Before accepting a role in a clinic, it's okay to ask:

- What kind of clients does the clinic attract?
- What values does the team hold around client care?
- How is workload managed, and how are bookings shared?
- How is communication handled—both with clients and between team members?
- What expectations are there around dress code, room use, time between clients?

These questions aren't just for your peace of mind—they help prevent misunderstandings and support healthy collaboration from the start.

You Still Need Boundaries

Just because you're part of a team doesn't mean you lose autonomy. You still get to decide:

- What techniques and modalities you offer

- How long your sessions run

- What you charge (depending on your arrangement)

- How you communicate with clients

Boundaries are just as important in a team as they are in private practice. And sometimes, they need to be even clearer. For example, you might need to speak up about needing enough time between bookings or not being expected to answer messages on your day off.

Your needs matter—even in a shared space.

Learning from Others (Without Losing Yourself)

One of the joys of working in a clinic is the chance to learn from colleagues. You might pick up new techniques, observe different communication styles, or see how others manage complex client situations.

But it's also easy to fall into comparison.

"They seem so confident."

"Their rebooking rate is higher."

"I should be more like them."

Pause. You bring your own strengths. You have your own style. You don't have to copy anyone to belong on the team.

Let it be a space for growth—but let that growth be your own.

Communication Is Everything

In any shared workplace, clear communication is the foundation of a healthy dynamic. That means:

- Checking in if something feels unclear or uncomfortable

- Being open about your needs and limits

- Respecting shared spaces, and asking for what you need to do your best work

- Being mindful of tone and timing—especially when tired or under pressure

You don't need to be perfect. But respectful, direct, and kind communication will take you far.

When It's Not the Right Fit

Sometimes, despite everyone's best efforts, a clinic just isn't the right match. Maybe the pace is too demanding. Maybe the style of care clashes with your values. Maybe you just don't feel at ease.

That's okay.

Leaving a clinic that doesn't feel right isn't a failure. It's part of refining your path.

"I've worked in three different clinics," one therapist shared, "and each one taught me something—about technique, teamwork, and what I really want. When I finally found the right fit, I knew, because I felt like I could breathe."

Therapist Story: Jamie Finds Her Voice

Jamie started her first role in a busy multi-modality clinic just two weeks after graduating. The rooms were beautifully set up, the admin staff were friendly, and the senior therapists seemed to really know their stuff.

But Jamie felt... small.

"I kept thinking "W*hy would anyone choose me when they could book the therapist with twenty years' experience down the hall?".* I was scared to ask questions. Scared to do things 'wrong.' I even apologised when I needed to take an extra five minutes to clean between clients."

At first, she tried to blend in, to copy the routines and scripts of others. But it didn't feel right. Jamie's sessions had always been a little slower, a little more intuitive. She needed more time to build trust with clients— and when she didn't allow for that, she left work feeling drained.

One day, after back-to-back sessions that had left her exhausted and anxious, Jamie spoke with the clinic manager. She explained she needed a longer gap between clients and wondered if she could update her bio to better reflect her style of work.

To Jamie's surprise, the manager said yes.

"Something clicked for me that day," Jamie said later. "I realised I didn't have to be like anyone else to be good at this. I could be me. And the clients who needed *that* would find me."

Over time, Jamie's confidence grew. So did her bookings.

"The clinic didn't change—but *I* did. I stopped trying to prove I belonged and started acting like I did."

Thriving in a Shared Practice

Let's take a moment to reflect on what kind of team or clinic environment would support you best.

What are my non-negotiables in a shared workplace? (Think about values, time between clients, communication, room use, etc.)

What would help me feel confident entering a new clinic? (Clear expectations, training, friendly introductions, a mentor?)

How do I want to contribute to a team dynamic? (What energy or mindset do I bring to shared work?)

What boundaries would help me stay grounded in a team setting? (Emotional, physical, energetic, or professional boundaries?)

How will I know when a clinic is a good fit for me?

Part Two: Designing Your Practice

Chapter 7: Vision and Workflow

Your practice, your way—from dream to day-to-day reality.

One of the most empowering things about being a massage therapist is that there's no single "right" way to run a practice. You get to shape your business—or your role within someone else's practice—in a way that reflects your values, energy, and goals.

But before you can set that in motion, you need a clear sense of your *vision.*

What kind of therapist do you want to be?

What kind of life do you want this work to support?

This chapter is about answering those questions—and then designing your workflow around what matters most to you.

Your Practice, Your Way

Some therapists want to see five clients a day, five days a week. Others want to work part-time alongside study, parenting, or another career. Some dream of opening their own wellness centre. Others want to rent a quiet room and keep things small and steady.

All of it is valid.

There's no prize for being the busiest. And your vision doesn't have to look like anyone else's. What matters is that it aligns with your energy, your needs, and your long-term wellbeing.

Let's make this practical.

Questions to Explore Your Vision

Grab a notebook or journal and jot down your responses to these questions—not to limit you, but to open possibilities:

- What kind of clients do I feel most drawn to working with?

- Do I want to work solo, as part of a team, or in a mix of environments?

- How many clients would I like to see in a typical week?

- What kind of energy do I want my clinic or work setting to have?

- What would a "successful" workday feel like, not just look like?

Let these questions shape your vision like a compass—not a cage. Your answers might shift over time. That's okay. But starting with clarity gives you direction.

Designing a Sustainable Workflow

Once you have a sense of your vision, it's time to look at your workflow. That's the rhythm of your day, your week, your systems—everything that makes your practice tick.

Start by mapping out your ideal week. Ask yourself:

- What days will I work with clients?

- When will I do admin, laundry, cleaning, and restocking?

- When do I need time off, quiet time, or family time?

- How much buffer time do I need between clients to feel calm and present?

You don't need to have every minute accounted for. But knowing your *ideal rhythm* will help you create healthy routines and protect your energy over the long term.

Your Workflow Will Evolve—And That's a Good Thing

You don't have to have it all figured out on day one. In fact, you *won't*.

You'll try things. You'll experiment. You'll realise you're more focused in the afternoons and need mornings off. You'll discover that four clients a day feels great—but five makes you cranky. You'll tweak, revise, and learn what works.

The key is to *keep checking in with yourself*. Ask, "How is this feeling?" and "What might need adjusting?"

This kind of self-awareness is one of the greatest gifts you can bring to your practice—and your clients will feel the difference.

Therapist Story: Flow Over Hustle

When Mia started her home-based practice, she thought success meant being fully booked all week. She packed in clients every day—often six or seven per day—and told herself she was "building momentum."

Within two months, her hands hurt, her sleep was disrupted, and she was constantly behind on laundry and admin. "I wasn't even enjoying the sessions anymore," she said. "I just felt like I was racing to keep up."

After a teary evening and a long chat with a mentor, she did something radical: she cleared her books for two weeks, raised her prices slightly, and started offering fewer appointments.

"I expected to lose clients," Mia said. "But what happened was—I started attracting the *right* clients. People who valued what I offered. And I started enjoying the work again."

My Practice, My Rhythm

Let's wrap this chapter with a few more questions to help you land your vision:

- What values do I want to guide the way I work?

- How do I want clients to feel when they walk into (and out of) a session?

- What would *burnout prevention* look like in my workflow?

- What do I want my practice to give me—not just financially, but emotionally and energetically?

Chapter 8: Choosing a Business Name and Identity

Finding a name that fits—and building a brand that feels like you.

What do you want people to think and feel when they hear your business name?

Something calm? Trustworthy? Modern? Nurturing? A little playful?

Choosing a business name is one of those steps that feels small but carries a lot of weight. It's often your first impression—on your website, on social media, on a business card handed over at a market stall or clinic reception. It can also shape the way *you* see your work.

So, let's take the pressure off and make this process feel creative and fun rather than overwhelming.

What Makes a Good Business Name?

There are no fixed rules, but here are a few helpful qualities to aim for:

- Memorable – Something that sticks in people's minds.

- Clear – Avoid names that are too vague or confusing.

- Relevant – It doesn't need to scream "massage therapist," but it should feel aligned with your services.

- Searchable – Think about whether the name is easy to Google, spell, and say aloud.

- Unique – Try to avoid names that are already in heavy use in your region or industry.

And here's a bonus one:

Personal – If it resonates with *you*, there's a better chance it will feel authentic to your clients, too.

Questions to Help You Brainstorm

Not sure where to start? Try journaling answers to these prompts:

- What three words describe how you want clients to feel after a session?

- Are there metaphors, images, or concepts that reflect your approach to healing?

- What values are at the heart of your work?

- What words or ideas are you naturally drawn to?

- What do people often say about working with you?

You might produce a name based on imagery (like "Still Waters Massage"), function ("Restore Therapy"), a feeling ("Ease and Flow"), or even your own name ("Massage by Taylor").

Let your ideas flow without censoring yourself at first. This is a creative process, not a test.

The Practical Side

Once you've got a shortlist of potential names, here are a few practical steps to take:

1. Search online – Is anyone else already using the name? Especially in your region or industry?

2. Check domain availability – If you want a website, can you get a version of the domain?

3. Check social media handles – Can you secure the same or similar names across platforms?

4. Look up your local business registration requirements – In Australia, for example, you'll need to register a business name with the Australian Securities and Investments Commission (ASIC) if you're trading under something other than your own name.

Even if you're not launching a website or marketing campaign right away, it's worth future-proofing your name a little.

Therapist Story: What's in a Name?

I originally named my practice "Bowen Therapy Adelaide," inspired by my original training in Bowen Therapy. It sounded professional, and I felt confident using it on flyers.

But then I obtained my Diploma in Remedial Massage. My business name no longer matched how I wanted to work. Firstly, many of my clients didn't know what Bowen therapy was and I found myself explaining it to them over and over. They also kept asking if I offer massage or other treatments. I also had no idea exactly where I wanted to base my clinic, so I didn't want to use a street or suburb name.

I rebranded.

"I changed the name to 'Remedial Therapies SA,' and everything shifted." "The clients who came in already knew what I was about. I didn't feel like I had to explain or justify anything—it just aligned."

Give Yourself Permission to Evolve

Your business identity is allowed to grow as you do. You don't have to get the "perfect" name straight away. You just need something that feels like *enough* to start.

You can always change it later. What matters most is that you begin— and that the name you choose feels like a warm handshake, an invitation, a tiny piece of your presence in the world.

Chapter 9: Setting Up Your Space and Systems

There's a beautiful moment that happens when your massage space is finally ready—the towels are folded, the oils are lined up, the room smells just right. It suddenly feels *real*. You're not just studying massage anymore. You're practicing. You're open for business.

But getting to that point can feel overwhelming. Where do you begin? What do you need? And how do you make sure it's all professional, welcoming, and within your budget?

This chapter will walk you through the practicalities of setting up your massage space and the systems that support it—whether you're working from home, renting a room, joining a clinic, or going mobile.

Choosing a Practice Location

Your location affects almost everything—your workday rhythm, your client experience, your costs, and even your energy levels. There's no one-size-fits-all answer, but here are the most common setups for massage therapists:

Working From Home

Pros:

- Low overheads
- Comfortable, familiar
- Flexible

Things to consider:

- Do you have a separate, private room?
- Are there council or landlord restrictions?
- How will you manage household noise or interruptions?
- Do you feel comfortable having clients in your personal space?

Renting a Room in a Clinic or Wellness Centre

Pros:

- Professional environment
- Opportunity for referrals
- Shared amenities

Ask about:

- What's included in rent?
- Your ability to decorate or personalise the room
- Booking and payment systems—who manages them?

Going Mobile

Pros:

- Flexible and often appreciated by clients
- Lower rent or setup costs

Think about:

- Transporting equipment (table, linens, supplies)
- Travel time and costs
- Safety considerations when entering private homes
- Setting clear boundaries for time, expectations, and locations

Co-Renting or Sharing a Space

Pros:

- Lower costs
- Camaraderie with another therapist

Requires:

- Excellent communication

- Clear agreements on cleaning, supplies, booking access

Your location doesn't have to be forever. Start where you are, with what's accessible, and grow from there.

Creating a Functional Treatment Space

Once you know where you're working, it's time to make the space yours—calm, clean, professional, and aligned with the kind of therapist you want to be.

Some key considerations:

- **Massage table**: Sturdy, adjustable, comfortable. (You'll be using it daily—invest wisely.)

- **Stool or chair**: For seated work and your own comfort.

- **Lighting**: Warm and soft, but still bright enough to work safely.

- **Music and scent**: These can shape the mood. Choose calming playlists, essential oils or subtle sprays that align with your brand and won't overwhelm. Be careful though, as music and scents can evoke strong emotions and not everything appeals to everyone. Sometimes it's best to go without.

- **Decor**: Keep it simple, uncluttered, and soothing. A few well-chosen pieces can make the space feel professional without being clinical.

You don't need to go overboard with decorations or equipment. Clients remember how they *felt* in your space far more than whether your diffuser was expensive.

Hygiene, Safety and Comfort

Your space needs to be clean, safe, and comforting—for your clients and for yourself.

Things to include in your setup:

- **Easy-to-clean surfaces** (and routines to clean them!)

- **Fresh towels and linens** for every client

- **Handwashing facilities** and hand sanitiser

- **Ventilation** for fresh air and hygiene

- **Temperature control**—especially if clients will undress

A small heater or fan can make a substantial difference. So can a blanket, bolster, or eye pillow to enhance comfort.

Daily Workflow

Your systems don't have to be complicated—but they do need to *work*.

Think about:

- **Start-of-day setup**: Do you lay out towels, check bookings, prepare oils?

- **Between clients**: What's your turnover routine? (Disinfecting, resetting the table, checking notes?)

- **End of day**: Tidying, laundry, prepping for tomorrow.

Having a clear routine can reduce decision fatigue and help you move through your day with ease.

Booking, Record-Keeping and Forms

Even if you're just seeing a few clients a week, it's worth setting up good admin habits now. They'll save you time, stress, and confusion later.

- **Booking system**: Whether it's a paper diary, Google Calendar, or online booking software, make sure it's easy for both you *and* your clients.

- **Client intake forms**: Include basic contact info, medical history, and consent to treatment.

- **Record keeping**: You're legally required (in Australia) to keep accurate client records for at least 7 years. Make sure they're stored securely and confidentially.

- **Progress notes**: Jot down anything relevant post-session—changes in condition, client preferences, areas of tension, etc.

Choose systems that are simple enough to maintain and professional enough to support your growth.

Policies and Procedures

You don't need a 40-page manual—but you do need to think through some foundational policies.

Common ones include:

- **Cancellation policy**: What's the notice period? Will you charge for late cancellations?

- **Refund policy**: Especially for pre-paid sessions or packages.

- **Cleaning policy**: How often do you disinfect surfaces, linens, and tools?

- **Linen policy**: How many sets do you need per day? Who does the washing?

- **Late arrivals/no-shows**: How do you handle them?

- **Scope of practice**: What do you treat, and what don't you treat? What happens if a client asks for something out of your scope?

Even if you don't share every policy with clients, having them clearly written down gives you clarity and confidence. And if you're working with others—roommates, team members, or contractors—clear policies protect everyone.

Therapist Story: Jo and the Sticky Notes

Jo had been in business for two weeks when he realised, he was drowning in paper: handwritten bookings, email enquiries, client notes scattered in three notebooks. He was spending more time *managing* his day than enjoying it.

"I sat down with a cup of tea, looked at all the sticky notes, and just started over. I signed up for an online booking platform and scanned all my client forms into secure digital folders. Now, everything's in one place and I'm not constantly worried I've forgotten something."

Start Simply, Grow Intentionally

Setting up your space and systems doesn't need to be perfect on day one. Start with what you have. Stay curious. Tweak as you go. Your systems exist to support you—not stress you out.

When your environment and routines are working *for* you, your energy is free to focus where it matters most: your clients, your wellbeing, and the growth of your practice.

What Does "Growth" Really Mean for Your Practice?

When we talk about "growth" in a massage practice, it's easy to think first about money. Of course, financial growth *is* important. You deserve to earn a living wage, to cover your expenses, to feel secure. It's perfectly fine to make "more income" one of your growth goals.

But growth isn't *only* about money. In fact, focusing solely on dollars can make you miss other signs that your business—and *you* as a practitioner—are growing in rich, sustainable ways.

So what else does growth look like?

Reaching Goals, Then Setting New Ones

Growth is about achieving what you set out to do—and then asking yourself, *What's next?* Maybe your first goal was to have five regular clients a week. Once you reach it, you might aim for ten. Or you might shift your goal to learning a new modality or refining your rebooking skills. Growth is the process of continuously evolving.

Improving Client Outcomes

Growth can mean helping clients see better results. Are you more confident in your assessments? Are you able to adapt treatments more precisely? Do clients tell you they feel better for longer? Those are *real* measures of professional growth.

Feeling More at Ease in Your Role

Remember when you were nervous about your first session? Growth often shows up as confidence. You trust your hands, your words, your boundaries. You know how to handle tricky client questions or special requests. You've moved from anxious to capable—and that's growth worth celebrating.

Consistency and Stability

Are you filling your calendar more reliably? Seeing more repeat clients? Feeling like you have systems that actually work? That steady, predictable business is a huge marker of growth. It's what turns your skill into a sustainable career.

Financial Progress

Of course, let's not downplay it. Growth can be charging a fairer rate, paying yourself regularly, or seeing your monthly income rise. It can mean moving from part-time to full-time massage work, or finally feeling like you don't need that second job. Money is an *important* signal—it just isn't the *only* one.

More Joy and Balance

Growth can look like *less* work if you want it to. Maybe you refine your practice to see fewer clients but give them more value. Or you learn to take time off without guilt. Maybe growth is taking a Friday off to watch your kids play sport, or having enough energy left at the end of the day to go for a walk. The proliferation of happiness in your life is a real and worthy measure of success.

Professional Development

Learning doesn't stop when you get your diploma. Growth might mean completing a short course, getting supervision, attending workshops, or reading or conducting research. Each new idea or technique expands your ability to help people—and keeps your work interesting.

Recognition and Trust

When other health professionals refer to you, when clients recommend you to their friends, when your reputation in your community grows—those are powerful markers of growth. They're signs you're not just *working*, but *valued*.

The Truth About Growth

There's no single benchmark you *have* to meet to call yourself successful. Growth is personal. It's about asking yourself: *What do I want my practice to look like? How will I know I'm moving in that direction?*

Maybe you want a busy clinic with a waiting list. Maybe you want a quiet, calm solo practice that pays the bills. Both are valid.

Your growth is defined by you. Don't let anyone else tell you what it should look like.

Setting Up Your Space and Systems – Checklist

Choosing a Practice Location

☐ A space that is quiet, private, and accessible

☐ Council or landlord approval (if required)

☐ Mobile setup packed and organised

☐ Clinic/room rental agreement reviewed and signed

☐ Insurance updated for chosen location

Treatment Room Setup

☐ Massage table (comfortable, adjustable, clean)

☐ Clean linens and towels (multiple sets

☐ Stools/chairs for therapist and client

☐ Blankets, bolsters, eye pillows

☐ Lighting (adjustable, calming)

☐ Music/sound system * in Australia you will need a OneMusic license to publicly broadcast copyrighted audio

☐ Scent/diffuser (if used)

☐ Decor that feels calm and professional

Hygiene and Safety

☐ Handwashing station or sanitiser

☐ Cleaning supplies (disinfectant, paper towel, gloves)

☐ Daily cleaning checklist in place

☐ Linens laundered and stored hygienically

☐ Waste bin with liner

☐ Ventilation/airflow considered

Workflow Systems

☐ Start-of-day setup routine

☐ Between-client reset plan

☐ End-of-day checklist

Client Management

☐ Booking system (paper, calendar, or online software)

☐ Intake forms (health history, consent, contact info)

☐ Treatment notes/documentation process

☐ Secure and private storage for client records

Policies and Procedures

☐ Cancellation and late arrival policy written

☐ Refunds and package policy (if relevant)

☐ Cleaning and linen procedures documented

☐ Privacy and confidentiality policy

☐ Scope of practice and referral boundaries

☐ Emergency contacts and safety protocol

Optional Extras

☐ Refreshments (water, herbal tea)

☐ Client welcome pack (intro note, aftercare, small gift)

☐ Branded items (uniform, towels, signage)

☐ Feedback forms or review prompts

Tip: Not everything needs to be perfect right away. Highlight or tick what's *essential* now and what you can work toward over time.

When I first started, I had a portable table, a single bolster, a pillow, and four sets of towels. Other items included flatpack shelving cubes, and two chairs.

Chapter 10: Essential First Purchases

What you need (and what you don't) to get started.

When you're just starting out, shopping for your massage practice can feel a bit like standing in the middle of a giant hardware store with no idea which tools you need. There's a lot out there—shiny gadgets, fancy oils, high-end extras—and it's easy to get swept up in thinking you need it *all*.

You don't.

You need the basics, thoughtfully chosen, to support great work and a sustainable workflow. The rest can come later, piece by piece, as your practice grows and your preferences become clearer.

Let's break it down.

Your Massage Table: The Heart of the Room

Your table is your foundation—literally. It's where your clients will rest, and where your body will move around hour after hour. This is one item where it's worth investing wisely.

Ask yourself:

- Do I need a portable or stationary table?

- What height range suits my posture and body mechanics?

- What thickness of padding feels best to *you* (test a few, if possible)?

- Do I want extras like a face cradle, armrests, or adjustable leg sections?

If you're working in multiple locations or doing mobile massage, portability and weight will matter. If you're setting up in a fixed clinic, stability and comfort might take priority.

My tip: Check for second-hand tables in good condition from reputable brands—many experienced therapists upgrade but take great care of their gear.

Linen & Towels: More Than Just Soft Stuff

You'll need enough linen to cover your busiest client days without running out. That usually means at least 3–4 sets of towels or sheets *per day* you plan to work, plus spares.

Think:

- Flat sheets or large towels

- Face cradle covers or hand towels

- Extra towels for bolstering

Quality matters, but so does easy washing and durability. Choose materials that can withstand frequent laundering and still feel lovely on the skin.

My tip: Start with neutral colours that don't show oil stains easily. (White looks nice—until it doesn't.)

Oils, Lotions & Hygiene Products

Every therapist has their personal favourite when it comes to what they use on skin. Some love unscented oils. Others swear by lotions or creams. You'll find your rhythm, but to begin:

- Choose 1–2 options you've trained with and trust.

- Look for products that are hypoallergenic, non-staining, and easy to dispense.

- Consider refill sizes to save money over time.

  And don't forget:

- Hand sanitiser

- Surface disinfectant

- Reusable cleaning cloths

- Gloves or masks (if applicable for your modality or client needs)

Hygiene isn't just about cleanliness—it communicates professionalism and safety.

Other Essentials

Depending on your setup, you may also need:

- A stool or chair for seated work or consultations

- A bolster or body cushion for support

- A small trolley or shelf to hold your products

- A laundry hamper with a lid (trust me on this one)

- A bin with a lid (and ideally with a pedal) for tissues and disposable items

- A lamp for soft lighting or dimmable lights in the room

These extras can help you create a calm, tidy, and comfortable treatment space—for both you and your clients.

Things You *Don't* Need Right Away

It's easy to get caught in the trap of "If I buy this, I'll look more professional." But a cluttered space or a strained budget doesn't help anyone.

You *don't* need:

- Dozens of essential oils or fancy diffuser systems

- Branded uniforms or fancy branded towels

- Pricey tech tools unless they're core to your modality

- More products than you can store and rotate regularly

Start simple. Let your experience and client needs guide you.

Therapist Story: Naomi's "Just Enough" Kit

Naomi was overwhelmed by all the shopping lists online when she finished her diploma. "I thought I needed to order everything right away—like if I didn't have a cupboard full of oils, I'd be seen as unprofessional."

Instead, she took a breath. She bought one great table, four towel sets, a bolster, and two small bottles of her favourite oil. That was it.

And guess what? "It was enough. I added things slowly as I realised what *I* needed, not what someone else told me was essential."

Reflect & Journal: My First Purchases

Before you start buying, pause and reflect:

- What kind of treatments do I plan to offer first?

- How many clients do I expect to see per day or week?

- Where will I store and launder my towels?

- What items do I already own or have access to?

- What can I borrow or buy second-hand while I get started?

Essential Equipment Planning Worksheet

For setting up your massage practice simply and confidently

Step 1: What I Already Have

List any items you've already purchased or have access to:

Item	Condition/Notes
Massage table	
Towels/sheets	
Oils/lotions	
Stool/chair	
Bolster/body cushion	
Cleaning products	
Laundry/storage setup	
Lighting	

Step 2: Must-Haves to Start With

What are the essentials you *need* before seeing clients?

Item	Notes	Estimated Cost

Tip: Focus on quality over quantity. What will truly support comfort, safety, and professionalism?

Step 3: Laundry & Hygiene Planning

- How many towel/sheet sets will I need per working day?
- Where will I wash them?
- Where will I store clean linens?
- How will I dispose of used wipes or tissues?
- What's my plan for cleaning between clients?

Step 4: Wish List – Nice but Not Urgent

What would you *like* to purchase down the track?

Item	Why I Want It	Timeline

Remember: A calm, confident presence is more important than having all the gadgets. Build slowly, with care.

Chapter 11: Booking, Record-Keeping, and Client Management

Ok, this part might not be the most glamorous, but it's where so much of your ease and professionalism begins. Booking systems, client forms, and secure record-keeping might not be what drew you to massage therapy, but when they run smoothly, *everything* else becomes easier.

This chapter is all about creating systems that support your work, respect your clients, and protect your energy. Think of this as the scaffolding behind your calm, professional presence.

Booking Systems: Find What Works for You

Whether you're fully booked or just starting out, having a straightforward way for clients to book is essential. The system you choose depends on your comfort level, budget, and workflow.

You might choose:

- **Pen and paper:** Great for total control and simplicity—but can lead to double bookings or missed messages.

- **Google Calendar:** Handy and free, but not client-facing unless you use it with a booking tool.

- **Booking apps:** These manage appointments, reminders, and sometimes even payments. Popular options include:
  - **Acuity**
  - **Cliniko**
  - **Timely**
  - **Square Appointments**

Things to consider:

- Can clients book directly, or do you prefer to manage it yourself?

- Do you need buffer time between sessions?

- Do you want to require deposits or prepayment?

- How do you handle cancellations or reschedules?

Whichever method you use, be consistent. Your clients will feel more confident when your process is clear and predictable.

Client Intake: Gathering the Right Information

Your first impression begins before the first massage. An intake form not only gathers essential health and contact information—it sets the tone for trust, safety, and collaboration.

Your intake form should include:

- Full name, date of birth, contact details

- Emergency contact

- Medical history, medications, injuries

- Contraindications (e.g. pregnancy, circulatory issues)

- Areas of focus or goals for treatment

- Consent to treat

- Acknowledgement of your policies

Some therapists use paper forms, while others prefer digital versions. There is no right or wrong, and one is not better than the other. The best is what works for you.

Remember, forms aren't just paperwork—they're communication. Keep the language kind, clear, and professional.

Treatment Notes: Why They Matter (Even If You Think You'll Remember)

It's tempting to think, *"I'll remember this client's neck tension issue next time."* But with a few weeks (or dozens of clients) between visits, memory fades.

That's why treatment notes are gold.

Your notes should include:

- Date of treatment

- Presenting issue or goal

- Techniques used

- Client's response

- Any changes observed

- Follow-up or recommendations

Not only do notes help you provide better care, but they're also important legally. In the case of an insurance claim or dispute, thorough notes can protect both you and your client.

You can handwrite notes and store them securely or use digital platforms with privacy protection.

In Australia, client records must be kept securely for a minimum of 7 years from the last entry. If the client is under 18, the requirement extends until they reach the age of 25.

Confidentiality and Secure Storage

Privacy is important—ethically, professionally, and legally. Your clients are trusting you with their stories and sensitive health information.

Make sure to:

- Store physical records in a locked cabinet

- Use password-protected digital tools

- Avoid discussing client cases outside your professional environment

- Have a clear confidentiality statement in your consent form

If you use a cloud-based system, ensure it meets privacy standards for your country (e.g. Australian Privacy Principles).

Managing Follow-Ups and Rebooking

Many clients benefit from regular massage, but they don't always know when to come back—or they forget.

Part of excellent client care is gently guiding them.

Try saying:

"Based on what we worked on today, I'd recommend coming back in two weeks. Does that suit you?"

Or:

"You're welcome to rebook now, or feel free to contact me when you're ready—I'll make a note to check in if I don't hear from you."

Some therapists use automated reminders or follow-up emails. Others send a personalised message a week or two later. Find a style that matches your voice.

Receipts and Record-Keeping for Claims

If you're registered with private health funds or offering claims (like through Work Cover), you'll need to issue receipts with:

- Your name and provider number
- Business name and ABN
- Date of service
- Amount charged and paid
- Duration of the session
- Description of service (e.g., "Remedial Massage")
- Client name

Even for general clients, providing clear receipts builds trust and helps them keep track of their wellness investments.

Systems That Support You

Your client management systems should feel like a supportive assistant—not another thing to stress about.

Start with what's simple. Add more structure as your practice grows. And if you're ever feeling overwhelmed, go back to this core question:

"How can I make this easier for me, and clearer for my clients?"

You don't need to have it all perfect from day one. But every step you take toward consistency and clarity makes your practice stronger.

Building Systems That Work

1. Booking System Checklist

Which system do you currently use (or plan to use)?

☐ Paper diary

☐ Google Calendar

☐ Booking app (which one?): _____

☐ Other: _____

Do you want clients to book themselves?

☐ Yes, I prefer automated booking

☐ No, I like to manage bookings manually

☐ I'm not sure yet

Do you need to include:

☐ Buffer time between clients

☐ Cancellation policy reminders

☐ Intake forms

☐ Deposit or prepayment

☐ SMS or email reminders

Next steps:

_____

_____

_____

2. Intake and Consent

What information will you collect before a client's first session?

☐ Contact and emergency details

☐ Medical history

☐ Presenting issues

☐ Goals or preferences

☐ Consent to treat

☐ Acknowledgement of clinic policies

Will your intake form be:

☐ Paper-based

☐ Digital (form link or built-in app)

How will you review it before the session?

_____

3. Treatment Notes

How will you record your treatment notes?

☐ Pre-printed form

☐ Digital notes or app

☐ Other: _____

What's your plan for keeping them secure and confidential?
☐ Locked cabinet

☐ Password-protected file or system

☐ Secure cloud system

☐ I need to research this more

---

4. Follow-Up and Rebooking

What feels natural for you when suggesting rebooking?
Write out a sentence you could use:

Would you like to send:

☐ Appointment reminders

☐ Follow-up texts or emails

☐ A thank-you message

☐ None of the above

Rebooking plan:

---

5. Client Files and Receipts

Do you know your legal record-keeping requirements?

☐ Yes

☐ No (add to to-do list)

How will you issue receipts?

☐ Printed or handwritten

☐ Automatically via booking software

☐ Emailed manually

What will your receipts include?

☐ ABN and business name and address

☐ Provider number (if applicable)

☐ Date, service (include time), cost

☐ Client full name

☐ Description (e.g., 1-hour Remedial Massage)

---

6. Notes to Self

What's working well with your admin systems right now?

What feels clunky, frustrating, or confusing?

One change I can make this week to improve my client systems:

Chapter 12: Policies, Procedures, and the Quiet Power of Clarity

At first glance, clinic policies might seem like just another bit of admin. But the truth is, a well-thought-out set of policies is like a quiet backbone for your business. It supports *you*, it protects your *clients*, and it keeps your practice running with fewer hiccups and more confidence.

Policies and procedures aren't about being rigid or impersonal—they're about setting expectations clearly and kindly, so everyone feels safe, respected, and on the same page.

Why Policies Matter More Than You Think

In those early months of practice, it can feel awkward to enforce boundaries. You might be tempted to waive your cancellation policy "just this once" or stay back late to squeeze someone in. But over time, this leads to burnout, blurred lines, and a business that feels like it's running *you*.

Policies give you something to refer to—not just for clients, but for yourself.

They say:

- "Here's how we do things here."
- "I respect your time, and I respect mine."
- "Let's keep this space clear, fair, and kind."

The Essentials: What Policies to Have

Your policies don't need to be long or legalistic. They just need to be clear, consistent, and communicated up front.

Here are the most common ones to consider:

1. Cancellation and Late Arrival Policy

What happens if a client cancels with short notice, or doesn't show up?

Example:

"Cancellations made with less than 24 hours' notice may incur a fee of 50% of the session cost. No-shows will be charged in full. I understand life happens and appreciate as much notice as possible."

2. Refund Policy

If a client is unhappy, gets called away, or forgets their appointment— what do you offer?

Be clear about:

- Whether you offer refunds at all
- How prepaid sessions are handled
- What happens with gift vouchers

3. Cleaning and Hygiene

Especially post-COVID, clients value knowing how you manage cleanliness.

Include:

- Fresh linen every client
- Hand-washing or sanitising requirements
- What you expect from sick clients (e.g., to reschedule)

4. Linen Policy (if relevant)

Do clients need to bring their own towel? Are you supplying all linen? What happens if something is soiled or stained?

Keep it simple and clear.

5. Privacy and Confidentiality

Let clients know how their information is stored and used.

Example:

"All client records are stored securely and confidentially. Your personal details and treatment notes are never shared without your permission, unless legally required."

6. Complaints Policy

Having a clear, professional complaints policy isn't about expecting things to go wrong—it's about showing your clients that you genuinely care about their experience. It reassures people that if they're unhappy or uncomfortable, they know exactly *how* to tell you and *what will happen next*.

Your policy should be simple, clear, and easy to share (for example, on your website, in your client intake forms, or on a visible notice in your room). It might include:

- **How** clients can make a complaint (verbally, in writing, via email).

- **What happens next**—for example, that you'll acknowledge the complaint within a certain timeframe.

- **How you'll work to resolve issues**, with fairness and respect.

- **That you'll keep a confidential record of complaints** for your own professional accountability.

- **Your membership details** if you belong to a professional association that offers a formal complaints pathway.

It's also good practice to mention that clients can contact external bodies if they feel their complaint hasn't been handled appropriately. In Australia, for example, many states and territories have Health Care Complaints Commissions or Ombudsman services that oversee health service providers. These government bodies provide an impartial, formal avenue for clients to raise serious concerns about health practitioners.

Having a clear policy isn't just ticking a box—it helps you stay calm and professional if a complaint ever arises, and it shows clients you respect them and take your responsibilities seriously. It's part of building trust, setting boundaries, and maintaining a reputation for integrity.

Procedures: Your Behind-the-Scenes Flow

A procedure is just a step-by-step way you do something in your practice. These aren't always shared with clients—but they help you stay consistent, especially when you're tired or stressed.

Some useful procedures to write out for yourself:

- Opening and closing your clinic each day
- Setting up your treatment room
- Cleaning between clients
- Managing late arrivals
- Responding to enquiries
- Handling complaints professionally

You can jot these in a notebook or keep them in a digital folder. Over time, they become your own "operations manual," especially helpful if you ever hire staff or take time off.

Therapist Story: Annie's Policy Wake-Up Call

Annie started her practice without a cancellation policy. "I wanted to be easy-going and flexible," she said. But within two months, she'd had five no-shows, and a few people cancel at the last minute.

"It wasn't just the money—it was the disruption to my day, the waiting around, the wondering if I could've booked someone else."

She added a clear cancellation policy to her intake form and started confirming appointments with an automated reminder. Things settled almost immediately.

"It felt scary at first, but people respected it. Honestly, most of them expected it."

How to Communicate Your Policies

Don't hide your policies in the fine print. Make them easy to find and read. You can include them:

- On your website
- In your booking confirmation emails
- As part of your intake form
- On a sign in your clinic space

And when you talk about them, keep it kind:

"These are just here to help things run smoothly and fairly for everyone."

Policies Are Kindness in Action

It's not about being strict—it's about being *clear*. Boundaries make your space feel safer, more professional, and more sustainable.

Good policies say to your clients:

"I respect you. I respect myself. I want our work together to feel easy and supportive for both of us."

Checklist: Creating Your Clinic Policies & Procedures

Core Policies

Go through each of the following and tick when you've created a clear version in your own words.

Cancellation Policy

☐ I've decided how much notice is required for cancellations

☐ I've set a fee (if any) for late cancellations or no-shows

☐ I feel confident explaining this to clients

Refund Policy

☐ I've decided whether I offer refunds

☐ I've written a clear refund process (especially for prepaid sessions or vouchers)

☐ I know how to handle awkward situations kindly but firmly

Cleaning and Hygiene Policy

☐ I've outlined how I clean between clients

☐ I've created a plan for what to do if I (or a client) is unwell

☐ My approach is practical and easy to follow

Linen Policy

☐ I know whether I supply all linen or ask clients to bring their own

☐ I have a process for managing soiled linen

☐ I've made this clear in my welcome or booking info

Privacy and Confidentiality Policy

☐ I store client records securely (physically and/or digitally)

☐ I've written a short confidentiality statement

☐ I know how long I need to keep client records (7 years minimum in Australia, or until age of 25 if client is a minor)

Complaints Policy Checklist

☐ I have described *how* clients can make a complaint. (e.g., in person, in writing, via email)

☐ I have informed clients how quickly I'll acknowledge or respond to their complaint. (e.g., "within 3 business days")

☐ I have explained what I'll do to investigate or address the concern.

☐ I have a system for securely recording complaints and my responses.

☐ I have told clients their complaint will be kept confidential and handled respectfully.

☐ I have included information about my professional association's complaints process.

☐ I have mentioned that clients can also contact relevant government agencies or health complaints bodies if needed.

☐ My policy is written in clear, client-friendly language (no confusing jargon).

☐ My policy is easy to find. (e.g., on my website, in my welcome pack, displayed in my clinic)

☐ The overall tone is respectful, professional, and reassuring—showing I genuinely welcome feedback.

Internal Procedures (For You)

These are optional to share with clients, but great for clarity behind the scenes.

Clinic Setup & Close-Down

☐ I've written down my opening/closing routine

☐ I have a checklist for cleaning and restocking

Client Flow

☐ I have a process for new client intake

☐ I know how I welcome and orient new clients

☐ I've written a checklist for what happens between clients

Late Arrivals / Rescheduling

☐ I have a plan for managing late clients

☐ I know how I'll handle rebooking in a way that feels respectful and clear

Enquiries & Bookings

☐ I have a script or template for responding to enquiries

☐ I use a booking system that supports my workflow

Complaints or Feedback

☐ I've considered how I'll manage feedback (both positive and difficult)

☐ I know what support is available if needed (e.g., association, mentor)

Sharing Your Policies with Clients

☐ My policies are included in my intake form

☐ My website or booking system displays my key policies clearly

☐ I've set up automated reminders or info emails if applicable

☐ I feel comfortable explaining my policies in person

Notes & Reflections

Which policy area do I feel most confident in?

Which one needs a little more thought or clarification?

One small step I can take this week to feel more prepared:

Part 3: Foundations and Frameworks

Chapter 13: Business Structures – Sole Trader, Employee, Contractor

When you're entering the profession, one of the biggest decisions you'll face is *how* you want to work. You might be offered a job in an established clinic. You might rent a room or decide to work for yourself. You might even do a bit of everything.

Each path—sole trader, employee, or contractor—comes with different responsibilities, risks, and freedoms. And none is inherently "better" than the other. What matters is that it fits your goals, values, and circumstances.

Let's break it down in real-world terms—no jargon, no business degrees required.

Sole Trader: Running Your Own Show

As a **sole trader**, you're self-employed. You run your own business, pay your own tax, and manage everything—from marketing to appointments to your super contributions. It's the most common setup for massage therapists in Australia.

You're responsible for:

- Registering an ABN
- Setting your own prices and schedule
- Managing bookings, payments, and cancellations
- Paying your own tax and super
- Your own insurance and compliance (e.g. provider numbers, association membership)

It's great if you:

- Want full control over your time and workflow
- Like creating your own brand or niche

- Don't mind the admin and learning curve

- Want to grow at your own pace

Employee: Working Within a Clinic or Organisation

If you're hired as an **employee**, the business takes care of many things for you. You're on their payroll, get regular hours (or a casual roster), and they pay your super and tax.

The clinic is responsible for:

- Providing the space, equipment, and supplies

- Handling advertising and bookings

- Paying you for hours worked

- Covering tax, super, and insurance

- Providing leave entitlements (if permanent)

You're responsible for:

- Showing up for shifts

- Providing quality care

- Maintaining professional standards

It's great if you:

- Want structure and a steady income

- Prefer to focus on massage without managing a business

- Are just starting out and want to learn within a team

- Don't want to stress about client acquisition

Contractor: Somewhere in Between

A **contractor** is technically self-employed but works *within* someone else's business. You might be paid per treatment or rent a room and bring your own clients. This is common in many massage and wellness clinics.

But here's the tricky bit: sometimes businesses **call** someone a contractor when legally, they should be an employee. The ATO has strict guidelines on this, and it's worth getting familiar with them.

As a contractor, you're likely responsible for:

- Holding your own ABN and insurance

- Paying your own tax and super

- Supplying your own equipment or linen (sometimes)

- Following clinic policies, while still being your own business

You may or may not:

- Set your own hours

- Bring your own clients

- Handle your own rebooking

It's great if you:

- Want flexibility but don't want to rent your own space

- Are building your client base with some support

- Are okay with less predictability in income

Which One Is Right for You?

There's no perfect answer—it depends on your goals, lifestyle, financial needs, and how much responsibility you're ready to take on.

Try asking yourself:

- Do I want to focus purely on massage, or do I enjoy the business side too?

- How much control do I want over my time, branding, and pricing?

- What level of income stability do I need right now?

- Am I ready to take on tax, insurance, and admin tasks?

You might start as an employee and shift into private practice later. You might rent a room and love it. You might be a contractor and run your own mobile practice on the side. It's okay to evolve.

Watch Out For...

If you're offered a contractor position, make sure to read the fine print. If the clinic:

- Sets your hours,

- Provides all equipment,

- Controls pricing and rebooking,

- But doesn't pay super or tax...

that could be a **sham contracting** arrangement, and it's not legal.

Don't be afraid to ask questions or seek advice. Your association or the Fair Work Ombudsman can help.

Growing into Your Role

No matter which structure you choose, **this is your career, not just a job**. It's okay to change paths as you grow. What works in your first year might feel restrictive or unsustainable later. Or you might find you love the steady rhythm of clinic work and never want to deal with BAS statements. That's valid too.

Choose what gives you the right balance of security, creativity, and sustainability.

Chapter 14: Licensing, Permits & Legal Essentials

Yes, it's a bit admin-y. But it's also the stuff that keeps your business protected, running smoothly and above board.

When you're launching your massage practice, one of the least glamorous but most important steps is sorting out the legal and regulatory pieces. And while it might feel overwhelming at first, this part doesn't have to be hard. Think of it as setting up the scaffolding that holds your work together.

When people imagine starting their massage business, they often picture the treatment room: warm lighting, calm music, and the quiet satisfaction of helping someone feel better.

What they don't imagine—at least not with as much enthusiasm—is emailing the council about parking regulations, registering for an ABN, or scrolling through insurance fine print at 11 p.m.

This chapter will walk you through the core admin tasks: licenses, permits, insurance, and keeping the local council happy. We'll also cover some of the key legal must-knows for Australian practitioners—so you can move forward with confidence (and fewer nasty surprises).

Registering Your Business

If you're setting up as a **sole trader** (which most massage therapists do when starting out), the first thing you'll need is an **ABN – Australian Business Number**.

You can register for free at: abr.gov.au

It's quick, and you'll need it for things like issuing receipts and applying for provider numbers.

You'll be asked to describe your business activity—select something like *massage therapy services* or *complementary health services*.

Once you have your ABN, you can:

- Legally operate as a business

- Invoice clients

- Register for provider numbers

- Apply for memberships with associations

Optional: You can also register a business name (if you're trading as something other than your own name), through ASIC at asic.gov.au. There's a small annual fee, but it protects your name. If you're trading under your own name (e.g., *Sarah Black – Remedial Massage*), you don't need to register a business name. But if you want to operate as *Vital Flow Bodywork* or *Calm Nest Therapy*, then you'll need to register that name with ASIC.

Council Permits and Local Requirements

Every local council in Australia has its own rules. And the last thing you want is to start seeing clients from home only to receive a polite-but-firm letter saying you're in breach of zoning laws.

It depends largely on **where you're practising** and **what kind of space** you're using.

If you're working from home:

If you plan to set up a clinic space in your house—whether it's a dedicated room, studio in the backyard, or converted garage, you'll likely need to apply for a **home-based business permit** through your local council. Some councils require this if you:

- Have clients visiting your home

- Put up signage

- Employ staff

- Make structural changes to the property

Even if you're just using a spare room for a few clients a week, it's worth calling your council and asking:

"Do I need a home-based business permit for a massage therapy practice?"

Also ask about:

- Parking regulations - Is there safe and adequate parking for clients nearby?
- Maximum client numbers per day/week
- **Noise restrictions:** Especially relevant if you're playing music or using equipment
- Signage restrictions - Some councils limit the size or visibility of business signs
- A **development approval** (for structural changes or signage)

Each council is different. Some allow you to see a few clients per day with minimal paperwork. Others require a full application process, including:

- A site plan
- Parking arrangements
- Waste disposal plans
- Neighbour notification

Ask for a confirmation email and keep it in your records.

Also make sure you ask the council about permission to practice dry needling, and requirements for safe needle disposal if this is a service you are intending to offer.

If you're renting a commercial room:

Check if the space is zoned for "health services" or "personal care." The landlord usually handles this, but don't assume—it's worth double-checking.

If the premises is shared (e.g., in a wellness centre), you may not need a separate permit, but **you're still responsible for compliance** in your own practice.

If you're working in a rented room or wellness centre:

- Make sure the premises are zoned appropriately (look for "personal services" or "health services")

- The building owner should already have permits in place, but don't assume—ask to see them

- If you're subletting, make sure your contract covers liability and expectations

Always keep written records of any communication with council. If someone tells you over the phone you don't need a permit, follow up with an email confirming that advice. It's handy if rules ever change.

Insurance – Non-Negotiable

Massage therapy is a hands-on, high-trust profession, but even when you work with care and professionalism, things can go wrong—clients can have unexpected reactions, trip over your doormat, or misunderstand your intentions.

You need to protect yourself and your clients. Most associations will require insurance before you can become a member or get a provider number.

That's why insurance is not optional—it's part of your duty of care and a requirement for provider numbers and most professional associations.

You will typically need two types of cover:

Professional indemnity insurance. This covers you in case a client claims your treatment caused them harm, or your advice led to an injury or worsening condition.

Public liability insurance. This covers accidents on your premises—like someone slipping on wet tiles, tripping over your door mat, or being injured by faulty equipment.

You can usually purchase both as a **combined policy**, often at a discounted rate through your association (e.g., Massage & Myotherapy Australia, ATMS, ANTA).

Check the fine print:

- What's the cover amount?

- Are you covered for all the modalities you offer?

- Are mobile treatments included, if you travel?

Some therapists also require **product liability** cover if they sell or use oils, balms, or heat packs.

Record-Keeping and Legal Minimums

Under Australian regulations, health practitioners (including massage therapists) are legally required to keep:

- **Client records** for **at least 7 years** (or until age 25 for minors) from date of last treatments

- **Receipts and business records** for **5 years** for tax purposes

Records must include:

- The client's full name and contact details

- Date and time of each session

- Notes on presenting issues, assessment, and treatment provided

- Consent (initial and ongoing)

- Any adverse reactions or referrals

Storage must be secure:

- Physical notes should be stored in a locked cabinet

- Digital files should be password-protected or encrypted and backed up

- Access should be limited to you (or authorised team members if in a clinic)

And yes—receipts count too!

The ATO requires you to keep financial records for **at least 5 years** for tax purposes.

Always have a backup system, especially for digital records.

Health and Safety Basics

Even as a solo therapist, you're responsible for providing a safe, hygienic space.

You may be audited or inspected, especially if offering services through private health funds.

You'll need to maintain:

- A clean, hygienic environment
- Access to hand-washing facilities and hand sanitiser
- A process for fresh linen between clients
- Safe storage of equipment and products
- A plan for cleaning high-touch surfaces regularly
- Follow infection control practices (especially if treating immunocompromised clients)

If you're renting a room in a shared facility, make sure you know who is responsible for shared space cleaning, laundry, and infection control.

Some associations offer checklists and infection control guidelines—especially post-COVID.

A Word on Scope of Practice

Massage therapists in Australia are considered **unregistered health practitioners**, meaning we are not part of the AHPRA system (like doctors or physios), but still bound by national and ethical standards.

In Australia, massage therapists work within a **self-regulated** system—usually under the guidance of a professional association. It's important to:

- Be transparent about your qualifications and scope

- Never claim to diagnose or treat medical conditions (unless qualified)

- Refer clients on if something is outside your training or comfort

- Maintain confidentiality and professional boundaries

- Work under a **code of conduct**, typically set by your association and your state or territory health regulations

If unsure, ask:

- Your association

- A trusted supervisor or mentor

- Your local state health complaints commissioner

Music License

Having permission to play music in a business setting is a legal requirement under the *Copyright Act (1968)*, regardless of what industry you operate in or how you play music. In Australia, if you intend to play copyrighted music, you will need a license to play music. You can apply for one by heading to https://onemusic.com.au

This Stuff Can Feel Intimidating

You're not alone if this makes your stomach turn a little. Most massage therapists don't get into the profession because they love paperwork.

At the same time, you don't just want to cross your fingers and hope for the best. You're setting up your practice to be **safe, compliant**, and **professional**—from day one.

It's not just for you. Clients feel it too. When your systems are smooth and your confidence is solid, your whole practice feels more grounded and professional.

Real-Life Perspective: Don't Skip This Step

Lucy was two years into running her clinic when she decided to expand. She rented a second room… only to discover her home didn't meet the council's zoning requirements for that level of commercial activity.

"It was a mess," she says. "I had to stop seeing clients for two weeks, get approvals retroactively, and pay a fine. I thought because I was small, I didn't need to worry about all that."

"The admin keeps your doors open and your stress low."

Displaying Your Qualifications and Registrations

It's a small detail that makes a big difference: displaying your qualifications, professional association membership, and any relevant registrations in your practice space helps build trust right away. It reassures clients they're in the hands of a trained, accredited professional. Whether it's a framed diploma on the wall, your association certificate at reception, or a simple mention on your website, these visible signs of your expertise show you take your role—and their care—seriously. It's a simple, effective way to boost credibility and create a welcoming, professional environment.

Quick Checklist: Am I Covered?

ABN and Registration

☐ I've registered my ABN

☐ I've registered my business name (if needed)

Local Council

☐ I've contacted my local council

☐ I've obtained necessary permits for my home or rented space

Insurance

☐ I hold valid professional indemnity and public liability insurance (check amounts required with your association)

☐ I understand my policy limits and what's included

Record-Keeping

☐ I securely store treatment and client records

☐ I'm clear on what I need to keep, and for how long

Health and Safety

☐ My space is clean, safe, and compliant

☐ I follow hygiene and infection control practices

Legal and Ethical Standards

☐ I know my scope of practice

☐ I'm a member of a professional association

☐ I've read the national Code of Conduct

Need more help?

Your association is often your best ally in all this. Most provide ready-made templates, checklists, and guidance. You don't have to reinvent the wheel—just customise it to fit your values and workflow.

Chapter 15: Choosing a Professional Association

It's more than just ticking a box—it's choosing your professional ally.

One of the first big decisions you'll make as a newly qualified massage therapist is which professional association to join. And while it might feel like a formality—just another step between you and your first client—it's a foundational part of your practice.

Your association isn't just about compliance. It's about connection, credibility, and ongoing support. It's the place you'll turn to when you have a tricky question, need up-to-date advice, want to register for CPE events, or need someone in your corner if something ever goes wrong.

And like any long-term relationship, it's worth choosing carefully.

Why You Need an Association

In Australia, massage therapists aren't part of a national registration scheme like AHPRA. Instead, we work within a **self-regulated framework**. That means we rely on **professional associations** to:

- Uphold standards of education and ethics

- Provide professional liability insurance (or access to it)

- Offer continuing education and professional development opportunities

- Help with provider numbers for health funds

- Represent our interests at national and state levels

- Offer advice when we're unsure what's required or expected

For clients, your association membership is a signal that you take your work seriously. For insurers and health funds, it's usually a **requirement** before they'll let you become a registered provider.

What to Look for When Choosing an Association

There's no single "best" association—it depends on your needs, values, and preferences. But here are some things to consider:

Recognition

- Is the association recognised by all the major health funds in Australia?

- Do they support the modalities you offer (e.g., remedial massage, myotherapy, lymphatic drainage)?

Support and Resources

- Do they offer templates for client notes, consent forms, and policies?

- Are there helplines or advisers you can contact when unsure?

- Do they provide regular updates about legislative changes or industry news?

Continuing Professional Education (CPE)

- Do they run their own events, webinars, or conferences?

- Do they accept a wide range of CPE providers and options?

Insurance Options

- Do they offer insurance bundled with membership?

- Is the policy flexible enough to cover all your services, including mobile or home-based treatments?

Community and Advocacy

- Do they actively advocate for the profession?

- Are they building relationships with government, health funds, and the public?

- Is there a sense of community—like networking groups, mentorship, or discussion forums?

Comparing the Big Names

Here are a few of the most well-known professional associations in Australia. This isn't an endorsement—just a starting point for your own research.

Massage & Myotherapy Australia (MMA)

- Offers insurance packages and provider number processing
- Strong focus on remedial massage and myotherapy
- Known for exacting standards and ongoing CPE opportunities
- Offers mentoring programs, support for new graduates

Australian Traditional-Medicine Society (ATMS)

- Covers a broad range of natural therapies, not just massage
- Useful if you plan to diversify into other modalities (e.g., aromatherapy, reflexology)
- Offers bundled insurance and regular CPE options

Australian Natural Therapists Association (ANTA)

- Known for stringent educational standards
- Strong advocacy for natural health professions
- Offers a more holistic approach to wellness professions

Each has different annual fees, requirements, and membership benefits. Take the time to read the fine print, compare inclusions, and even call and ask questions.

What I Looked for When I Started

When I chose my first association, I was mostly just trying to tick the boxes to get my provider numbers. I didn't really know what else to look for—and I didn't realise how valuable my association would become.

A year or so in, I reached out for advice on how to word a tricky consent form for a complex client. The person I spoke to was warm, calm, and practical. That call made me feel less alone in my work, and more confident in my ability to run a safe, ethical, client-focused practice.

These days, I see my association as part of my professional toolkit—not just a name on a certificate.

Tip: Ask Around

Chat with colleagues, mentors, or even people from your course. Ask:

- What do you like about your association?
- Have they been helpful when you've needed support?
- Is there anything you wish you'd known before joining?

You might also attend open information sessions or webinars that associations run for students and graduates.

Final Thought

Don't get too stuck in the weeds. The most important thing is to **choose one and join**—it's a critical step in making your practice real and ready. But do take the time to find a group that aligns with your values, supports your growth, and helps you navigate your professional world with confidence.

Over time, that relationship may grow and change—just like your practice will. And that's a good thing.

Choosing a Professional Association – Comparison Table

Feature/Benefit	Massage & Myotherapy Australia (MMA)	Australian Traditional Medicine Society (ATMS)	Australian Natural Therapists Association (ANTA)
Focus Areas	Remedial Massage, Myotherapy	Massage, Naturopathy, Aromatherapy, Reflexology	Broad natural therapies, incl. nutrition & massage
Insurance Options	Bundled options available	Bundled insurance through selected providers	Offers insurance packages through preferred insurers
Provider Numbers Support	Yes – Health fund provider processing	Yes – Health fund provider processing	Yes – Health fund provider processing
CPE Opportunities	Extensive in-house CPE, webinars & events	Offers external and internal CPE opportunities	Strong CPE support, including conferences
Modality Flexibility	Massage and Myotherapy focused	Wide range of natural therapies accepted	Multimodality focused – holistic approach
Student Support & Mentoring	Yes – mentoring and new graduate resources	Limited – varies by region	Limited – some mentoring programs available
Advocacy & Representation	Active at national and state levels	Longstanding presence in traditional medicine	Known for advocacy in natural and complementary health
Membership Fees (Approx.)	$220–$280/year + insurance	$200–$300/year + insurance	$200–$300/year + insurance
Reputation	Highly regarded in remedial massage	Broad, inclusive, established across modalities	Strong emphasis on education standards

Feature/Benefit	Massage & Myotherapy Australia (MMA)	Australian Traditional Medicine Society (ATMS)	Australian Natural Therapists Association (ANTA)
Ease of Contact & Member Support	Phone, email, responsive help	Phone, email, response times vary	Member portal + email support

Choosing What's Right for You

Use this table as a starting point. Your ideal association will depend on:

- What modalities you want to practise

- Whether you want all-in-one insurance and admin support

- The kind of community and growth opportunities you're seeking

Take a moment to reflect:

Do I want a focused massage association or one that supports multiple therapies?

Will I need mentoring, templates, or advocacy support?

Do I value access to events and conferences as part of my growth?

Chapter 16: Getting Provider Numbers

Opening the door to health fund rebates—and why it matters even if you don't think it does yet.

One of the most frequent questions new massage therapists ask is, *"How do I get provider numbers?"*—usually followed closely by *"Do I even need them?"*

The short answer? It depends on how you want to work.

Provider numbers allow your clients to claim rebates from their private health funds for eligible massage treatments. In Australia, this is particularly relevant for **remedial massage therapists** who meet the necessary qualifications and association requirements.

Not every therapist offers health fund rebates. But even if you're not sure you'll need them, it's usually worth going through the process—so the option is there when you decide to offer them.

Let's unpack it step-by-step.

What Is a Provider Number?

A **provider number** is a unique identification code that links you, your qualifications, your association membership, and your place of practice with a specific **health fund**.

Clients use this number when they submit a claim to their private health insurer for a rebate on your services. Without it, they can't claim—and that may be a dealbreaker for some clients, especially in areas where rebates are expected.

Important to note:

Unlike AHPRA-registered health professionals (like GPs or physiotherapists), massage therapists in Australia get **separate provider numbers for each health fund and each practice location**.

That means:

- If you work from two separate locations, you'll need provider numbers for both.

- If you change address or name, you'll need to update the funds.

It sounds fiddly—and it is. But once you get the hang of it, it's a manageable part of your admin routine.

Who Can Apply?

To be eligible for provider numbers with Australian health funds, you'll generally need:

- A **Diploma of Remedial Massage (HLT52015 or equivalent)**
- Membership with a **recognised professional association**
- **Current professional indemnity and public liability insurance**
- A **registered ABN** (Australian Business Number)
- A designated **business address** (home or commercial)

Some funds have additional criteria, like:

- A minimum number of face-to-face clinic hours in your training

- Recognition of the specific institution where you studied

- Evidence of continuing professional education (CPE) each year

It's your professional association that checks and certifies your eligibility—and often acts as the intermediary between you and the health funds.

Which Health Funds Offer Rebates?

This changes from time to time, as some funds alter or restrict their recognition of massage therapists.

As of now, some of the **main Australian health funds** that may offer rebates for remedial massage include:

- **Bupa**

- **Medibank Private**

- **HCF**

- **nib**

- **Australian Unity**

- **Teachers Health**

- **CBHS**

- **Police Health Fund**

Always check the latest information with your association. Some funds have ceased recognising new massage therapists or have changed their criteria.

How Do I Apply?

The application process typically goes like this:

1. Join a Professional Association

This is step one. Without an association, you won't be eligible for provider numbers. Most associations will verify your qualifications, insurance, and identity when you join.

2. Request Provider Number Forms or Access

Once you're a member, your association may:

- Automatically apply to certain health funds on your behalf

- Provide you with downloadable application forms or online portals for each fund

- Guide you through the paperwork (some even handle it for you)

Each health fund has different processes. Some use online portals. Others still require scanned forms and supporting documents.

3. Submit the Required Information

You'll typically need to supply:

- Your name, contact info, and ABN

- Your practice address(es)

- Proof of qualification (e.g. transcript or certificate)

- Insurance certificate of currency

- Details of your association membership

- Your modalities (must include remedial massage)

Some funds issue provider numbers quickly. Others may take weeks or even months.

4. Keep a Record of Everything

It's quite common for health funds to lose track of applications or miss details. Keep a spreadsheet or document with:

- Dates of submission

- Which numbers you've received

- Contact emails or confirmation numbers

It'll save you hours down the line.

Provider Numbers for Multiple Locations

If you work from more than one location—say, a clinic three days a week and a home studio on Saturdays—you'll need separate provider numbers for each address.

This is a common oversight, and it can lead to **client claims being rejected** if they use the wrong number.

If you move clinic locations or change your business name, you'll need to update the funds too. Some therapists set calendar reminders every 6 months to review their details across all health fund systems.

What If You're Working as a Contractor or Employee?

No matter how the clinic is set up, you still need your own provider number if you want clients to be able to claim from their healthfunds.

- If **you invoice under your own name and ABN**, and clients are booking with you directly, you'll need your own provider numbers if you want clients to be able to claim from their healthfunds.

- If **you're working under the clinic's name**, then you will still need your own provider numbers. Provider numbers belong to the individual therapist. It is illegal to use somebody else's provider number.

You will need a different provider number for each location you work at.

It is your responsibility to ensure your provider number is used correctly, and only for services provided by you. This is regardless of who issues the receipts. Remember to update any change in your details or add/cancel locations with your association and health funds.

Your provider number isn't just about rebates—it affects your professional identity and client trust.

What If You Don't Want to Offer Rebates?

That's okay. Some therapists choose not to be health fund providers because:

- They want to simplify their admin

- Their work is more holistic or doesn't fit health fund criteria

- They're focused on niche, private-pay clientele

- They want to avoid being associated with health fund limitations

You can still build a thriving practice without offering rebates. Just be clear in your advertising and conversations with clients so they know they can't claim.

"I don't offer health fund rebates, but my focus is on high-quality, tailored care that puts you—not your fund's requirements—at the centre of the session."

This is especially common for those working in integrative wellness spaces. It is important to still ensure you have adequate insurance cover.

A Note from Experience

My Association made the process easy, and I received my main Provider numbers within 4 weeks. A few smaller funds I had to approach myself and apply for a provider number. One of them was almost instant. I phoned them, gave my association membership number and it was sorted. The next one? Six months. They gave me a number but entered my name wrong, which led to every single claim being rejected until we fixed it.

It was frustrating. But I kept records, followed up kindly but consistently, and learned to build buffer time into my setup process.

The lesson?

This isn't a glamorous part of practice—but it is a powerful one. For many clients, being able to claim makes massage accessible. For therapists, provider numbers add a layer of legitimacy, structure, and flexibility to your business.

Chapter 17: Contracts and Agreements

Getting clear, staying protected, and avoiding awkward surprises.

When you're starting out in massage therapy—whether as a solo practitioner, contractor, or employee—it's tempting to go with the flow. You might think, *"We're all on the same page,"* or *"It's just a handshake agreement—I trust them."*

But here's the truth: clarity protects relationships. A good contract isn't about mistrust. It's about making sure everyone knows what's expected and agreed upon. It prevents awkwardness, resentment, and confusion down the track.

This chapter will help you understand what kinds of agreements you may need, what to look out for, and when to get help.

Why we need Contracts

In massage therapy, we often think of our work as personal, even intimate. We're in helping roles, and many therapists are naturally generous. But that doesn't mean we should be vague about money, hours, or expectations.

Whether you're:

- Renting a room
- Working in someone else's clinic
- Taking on a contractor role
- Hiring staff
- Subletting space in your home practice

You need to define the terms of your working arrangement—on paper.

"But they're lovely—I'm sure it will be fine."

That's great—until something changes. Maybe they sell the business. Or you want to reduce your days. Or the rent increases. A written agreement gives you something to refer to when memories or circumstances shift.

Common Types of Agreements

Here are the main types of contracts you may come across as a massage therapist:

1. Room Rental or Space Hire Agreement

If you're renting a room (in a wellness centre, clinic, or private practice), you'll likely sign a rental or licence agreement.

This should include:

- Days/times the space is available to you

- Rent amount and payment schedule

- What's included (utilities, towels, reception support, HICAPS machine, etc.)

- Access to shared facilities (toilets, waiting area, Wi-Fi)

- Termination policy (notice period required)

- Cleaning responsibilities and expectations

- Storage access or restrictions

Tip: Make sure it clearly says whether you're leasing a space as a business owner or being contracted as part of their business. It affects your responsibilities (and rights).

2. Contractor Agreement

If you're working as a contractor in someone else's clinic (common in massage), the contract should clearly outline:

- **Pay structure** (percentage split or flat rate)

- **Client ownership** (Do you keep your clients if you leave?)

- **Booking and cancellation policies** (Who handles them?)

- **Payment schedule** (When and how are you paid?)

- **Marketing expectations** (Do you promote yourself, or do they?)

- **Supplies and linen** (Who provides what?)

- **Professional standards** (Dress code, hours, admin systems)

Many contractor roles operate under an ABN arrangement, so you're technically running your own business under their roof.

Warning: Some clinics call you a "contractor" but treat you like an employee—controlling your hours, rates, or holidays. This is a legal grey area and can affect your tax, insurance, and superannuation. If unsure, get advice.

3. Employment Agreement

If you're employed (less common in massage), you'll likely have:

- A regular wage (hourly or salary)

- Superannuation

- PAYG tax deducted

- Sick leave and holiday pay

- Clear rosters or scheduled hours

- Set expectations around dress, duties, breaks

This is often more structured but less flexible than contracting, but remember you still need professional liability insurance.

4. Subletting or Sharing Agreements

If you're offering space in your clinic or home studio to another therapist, protect yourself with a simple agreement.

Cover:

- Rent amount and due dates
- Use of facilities and equipment
- Policies on keys, security, and cancellations
- Code of conduct (especially if you're sharing clients or staff)
- Conflict resolution process

Even if you're friends now, life changes. It's easier to work things out if you've got the basics agreed in writing.

What to Look Out For

Before signing anything, check for:

- Clear definitions of roles
- Specific terms about pay, rent, and responsibilities
- Termination clauses (notice periods, grounds for ending agreement)
- Conditions around client files and privacy
- Flexibility or restrictions on seeing clients outside the clinic
- Non-compete or restraint clauses (some are enforceable, some aren't—but they're always worth understanding)

Should I Get Legal Advice?

Not every agreement needs a lawyer—but it never hurts to have someone look over a contract before you sign it, especially if:

- The terms seem overly restrictive

- You're investing a lot (e.g., building a room, buying stock)

- You're unsure what certain clauses mean

Some professional associations offer **free or discounted legal reviews** for members—take advantage of this!

Personal Story

I once worked in a clinic where everything felt perfect—until I realised my contract didn't say what would happen if a client rebooked with me privately. When I left the clinic some months later, things got a bit awkward. Although I never told my clients of my new address (over 15kms away from the other one), a couple looked me up and found me anyway. It wasn't about stealing clients—it was about not having discussed it upfront.

Another thing that wasn't mentioned in the contract was who owned the client records.

A two-sentence clause in a contract could've saved both of us stress and assumptions.

Now? I clarify everything from day one. It keeps things cleaner, kinder, and more professional.

Questions to Ask Before Signing

- What exactly am I agreeing to do—and for how long?

- How is payment calculated and delivered?

- What happens if I want to leave or change the arrangement?

- Who owns the client records?

- Am I expected to do admin, cleaning, or reception duties?

- What happens if I can't work (e.g., due to illness or injury)?

- Are there any restrictions on seeing clients elsewhere?

Write these down. Ask them. Trust your gut—but back it up with good documentation.

Chapter 18: Financial Systems and Setting Prices

Money matters—and so does the way you manage it.

When you're starting out as a massage therapist, you're often filled with energy for the hands-on part of your work—but the financial side? That can feel overwhelming, boring, or even scary.

But here's the truth: having solid, simple financial systems in place is one of the most empowering things you can do. It gives you clarity, confidence, and control. And setting your prices well? That's not about greed—it's about sustainability.

Let's dive in.

Setting Up Your Financial Foundations

You don't need to be a spreadsheet wizard or an accountant to run a financially healthy practice. But you do need a few clear systems from the start.

1. Separate Your Money

Open a dedicated business bank account—even if you're a sole trader.

This:

Keeps your business and personal finances clear

Makes it easier to track income and expenses

Helps you prepare for tax time (you'll thank yourself later)

If you're not ready for a full business account, consider a second personal account just for business use.

2. Track Your Income

This can be as simple or sophisticated as you like. The key is consistency.

Options include:

A basic spreadsheet (track date, client, service, amount)

A booking system with built-in reports (e.g. Halaxy, Cliniko)

Accounting software (Xero, QuickBooks, Rounded)

You'll want to track:

How much you earn

What services are most popular

No-shows or cancellations

Client rebooking rates (useful for goal setting!)

3. Record Your Expenses

From table oil to towels, everything you spend on your practice should be recorded. Other common deductible expenses:

Insurance

Professional memberships

Courses and CPD

Website costs

Business cards

Cleaning supplies

Equipment maintenance

Keep your receipts. Use a folder, a scan app, or accounting software.

4. Plan for Tax and Super

In Australia, if you earn over $18,200 as a sole trader, you'll need to pay tax. If you're earning over $75,000 per year, you'll need to register for GST.

Even if you're under those thresholds:

Put aside 20–30% of your income in a separate tax savings account

Consider voluntary super contributions (future-you will be grateful)

You may also be eligible for small business deductions—chat with a bookkeeper or tax agent familiar with sole traders.

Setting Your Prices with Confidence

Here's the big question almost every new therapist asks: **"How much should I charge?"**

There's no one-size-fits-all answer. Your pricing should reflect:

Your costs and time

Your location and market

Your level of skill and experience

The value you provide

Start With Your Costs

First, figure out your **minimum viable rate**—what you must charge to cover:

Rent

Insurance

Supplies

Tax

Admin time

Ongoing education

Sick leave and time off

Then, look at your ideal income and how many hours you realistically want to work. You might realise that $80 an hour won't cut it if you only want to treat fifteen clients a week.

Check Your Local Market

Look at what other therapists are charging—but don't just copy them. Think about:

What's included (time, extras, HICAPS)

Are they running a high-volume clinic, or a boutique solo space?

Do they offer rebates?

You don't need to be the cheapest. You need to be **clear, consistent, and confident**.

Pricing low to attract clients often backfires—it can undervalue your work, attract bargain hunters, and leave you burnt out.

Your Pricing Toolkit

Include in your pricing:

Treatment time (e.g. 60 mins hands-on + consultation)

Your preparation and admin time

Extra touches (hot towels, aromatherapy, post-treatment support)

Whether it's claimable under health funds

Be transparent on your website, in your booking system, and in conversations. Clarity builds trust.

As You Grow...

You might revisit your prices as your practice evolves. Signs it might be time to increase them:

You're booked out weeks in advance

You feel resentful or underpaid

You've invested in extra skills or training

You've improved your space, tools, or outcomes

Increasing your rates doesn't have to be scary. Most clients understand—and the right ones will stay.

A Personal Note

I remember the first time I raised my prices. My heart was in my throat when I sent out the SMS to existing clients. But not a single client questioned it—and a few even said, "It's about time!"

Money conversations get easier with practice. Think of it not as charging for time, but for **value**. You're offering not just touch, but trust, care, and transformation.

Something else I feel is worth mentioning – you don't have to justify your prices. In the beginning I felt I had to justify any increases. You really don't. The CPI, interest rates, everything else changes. Why not your prices.

Your Financial Checklist

- Open a separate account for business
- Track income and expenses (whatever system works for you)
- Set aside money for tax and superannuation
- Review your costs to guide pricing
- Communicate clearly with clients
- Revisit and revise your prices as needed

Setting Your Prices with Confidence

Step 1: Know Your Costs

Expense Type	Monthly Estimate	Notes
Clinic/Room Rent		Include electricity if not shared
Insurance (monthly avg.)		PI and public liability
Supplies (oils, linen)		Cleaning, oils, laundry, etc.
Booking System/Software		Halaxy, Cliniko, etc.
CPD/Training		Break down into monthly average
Marketing/Website		Hosting, domain, ads
Super Contributions		Recommended, even if optional
Tax Savings (30% approx.)		
Admin Time		Estimate weekly unpaid hours

Total monthly business cost: $ _____

Step 2: Map Out Your Week

- How many **clients** would you ideally see per week? _____

- How many **hours** per week do you want to work? _____

151

Now divide your **monthly costs** by the number of billable sessions per month to find your **minimum viable session rate**.

Minimum viable hourly/session rate: $ _____

You might realise that what seems like "a good rate" isn't sustainable once you add in taxes, breaks, and unpaid admin time.

Step 3: Consider Value and Positioning

Tick any that apply to your practice:

- I use high-quality products or extra touches (e.g., hot towels, music, oils)
- I have additional training or niche expertise
- I offer a calm, welcoming space
- I offer private health rebates
- I spend extra time before/after sessions with clients
- I am committed to sustainable, long-term practice

If most of these apply, **you're offering high value.** Make sure your prices reflect that.

Income Tracker Template (Sample Layout)

Date	Client Name	Service	Fee	Payment Method	Notes (e.g., rebate claimed?)
1/7/25	Sarah H.	60 min	$120	EFTPOS	Claimed HCF
2/7/25	Ben M.	90 min	$150	Cash	Loyalty client

Date	Client Name	Service	Fee	Payment Method	Notes (e.g., rebate claimed?)
...					

You can total these weekly, fortnightly, or monthly—whatever feels manageable for you.

Bonus: Sample Price Increase Notice (Email or Poster)

Subject Line: A Small Update to My Fees

Hi [Client's First Name],

Thank you for being part of my practice—it means the world to me.

From [Date], I'll be adjusting my session fees slightly to reflect rising costs and the value I continue to offer.

New fee structure:

• 30-minute session: $[new rate]

• 60-minute session: $[new rate]

This adjustment helps me sustain the quality of care, time, and resources I pour into every session. I genuinely appreciate your understanding and ongoing support.

If you have any questions, I'm always happy to chat.

Warmly,
[Your Name]

Or keep it simple. I do.

I put up a small sign next to my EFTPOS machine:

Please note that our prices will increase slightly as of [date]. Thank you for your ongoing support,

Part Four: Building Your Visibility

Chapter 19: Defining Your Brand

Who you are, how you show up, and why it matters.

Let's talk about what people see when they find you—online, in a directory, or on your business card. Let's talk about *who you are* in your practice, and how you want clients to experience that before they even walk through the door.

Branding might sound like something big companies do, but for small practices—especially massage therapists—your brand is personal. It's the feeling people get when they hear your name. It's the consistency between what you say, how your space feels, and how you show up in session.

You don't need a flashy logo or expensive website. You just need a clear, authentic message and a sense of identity that feels aligned with who you are and how you work.

It's how you build trust before someone even walks through the door.

And in massage therapy, where clients are putting their wellbeing—sometimes even their pain, trauma, or vulnerabilities—in your hands, trust is everything.

Who Are You in Practice?

Let's start with you.

What kind of experience do you *want* clients to have?

What three words would you love people to associate with your business?

How do you want to *feel* at work every day?

Maybe you want your practice to feel warm and nurturing. Or calm and clinical. Or confident and empowering.

There's no right answer—but knowing this helps shape every other decision.

Example:

Two massage therapists can both offer remedial massage—but if one's space is candle-lit and gentle, while the other's is energetic and functional, they're offering vastly different experiences. Both are valid. Both attract different people. That's the power of branding.

The Elements of a Personal Brand

Your brand is shaped by everything a client experiences. Here are just a few pieces that form the whole:

1. Your Visual Identity

This is the part many people jump to first. It's best to do *after* you know your brand values.

Your visual identity includes:

- **Logo** (simple, clean, readable)

- **Colours** (choose a palette of 2–3 that represent your tone)

- **Fonts** (something professional and easy to read)

- **Images** (photos or illustrations that reflect your space, tone, or niche)

There are plenty of free and affordable tools to help you build a brand kit—Canva, Looka, or even Etsy templates. You don't need to hire a designer unless you want to.

The key is **consistency**. Use the same colours, fonts, and tone across your website, flyers, business cards, and social media.

It doesn't have to be fancy, but it should feel *cohesive* and *true to you*.

2. Your Tone of Voice

Your "brand voice" is how you speak to your audience—whether it's in a social media post, a website intro, your signage, or a reply to a client email.

Some voices are calm and grounding. Some are quirky and fun. Some are very professional and structured. None are right or wrong. The goal is to speak how you speak—and to write in a way that feels natural to you.

3. Your Values

Do you value inclusivity? Evidence-based care? Relaxation? Precision? Do you work primarily with athletes, parents, queer communities, or desk workers?

Your values guide your language, your decor, your choice of images— They help clients decide if they resonate with you.

Your Brand Values and Message

Before you choose colours or fonts, ask yourself:

- What do I stand for?
- What do I want my clients to feel when they engage with me?
- What kind of people am I hoping to attract?

These values are the heart of your brand. Maybe you're all about gentle care and deep relaxation. Maybe you bring strength, structure, and anatomical precision. Maybe your focus is inclusivity, or trauma-informed care, or nervous system regulation.

Whatever it is, let it guide your messaging. When your brand reflects your values, clients are more likely to feel trust and alignment from the first interaction

Building a Brand That Reflects *You*

Your brand is already forming, whether you've officially "designed" it.

Ask yourself:

What kind of space have I created?

What do my social media posts say about me?

Would a stranger looking at my booking page understand what I offer?

Is there a consistent *feel* across my online and offline materials?

It's okay if the answer is "not yet." Branding evolves. You're allowed to refine and shift as you grow.

Common Myths About Branding

Myth 1: You need to hire a designer right away. Truth: You can start with Canva and a clear sense of your vibe. Keep it clean, readable, and aligned with your values.

Myth 2: You must sound professional and formal. Truth: Professional doesn't mean stiff. It means clear, respectful, and aligned with your audience.

Myth 3: Branding is only for Instagram therapists. Truth: Whether you work in a rural town or a wellness hub, people are making decisions based on how you present. Branding matters everywhere.

A Personal Note

When I first started, I thought branding was about being impressive. But the more I've grown in business, the more I've realised:

Good branding is about being *recognisable and real*.

You don't need to look like everyone else. Look and sound like *yourself*.

The clients who need you will feel that.

Your brand is more than a logo—it's the emotional and sensory experience of your business

It includes your tone, visuals, values, and how you show up in person and online

Strong branding helps clients self-select and builds trust before the first session

You don't need to have it all perfect to get started. Branding is allowed to evolve with you.

Therapist Story: Tasha's Rebrand

Tasha started out as "Soothe & Relax Massage," but something never sat quite right. Her treatments were deep, focused, and full of education. She realised she was attracting the wrong clients—people who wanted a pampering spa day, not therapeutic bodywork.

She rebranded as "TheraBody by Tasha," with a new tagline: *Movement. Recovery. Empowerment.* Her content shifted to reflect her real voice—strong, direct, and supportive.

"I didn't change my services," she says. "I just stopped pretending to be something I wasn't."

Aligning Brand and Practice

Your brand is everything the client sees before and after the session. It's not about being polished. It's about being *clear*.

If your brand is warm, gentle, and trauma-informed, that should show in your language, your intake forms, and your space. If you're analytical and rehab-focused, let that shine through in your tone and testimonials.

Your brand should feel like you. That way, the clients who book in are the ones who'll feel most at home with your work.

You Don't Have to Do It All Now

You can start with a basic logo (if you decide to use a logo), a name you like, and some consistent messaging. As your confidence grows, you'll refine your identity and adjust.

What matters most is that your brand feels true to who you are, where you're going, and the kind of people you want to help along the way.

Find your own Branding and Voice

1. What Do You Stand For?

What values are at the heart of your massage practice?
(Choose or write your own)

- [ ] Care and compassion

- [ ] Safety and trauma awareness

- [ ] Evidence-informed practice

- [ ] Relaxation and nervous system regulation

- [ ] Strength and resilience

- [ ] Empowerment and education

- [ ] Inclusivity and accessibility

- [ ] Other: _____

In your own words, what do you care most about in your work?

_____

_____

_____

2. Who Are You For?

Who is your ideal client? Who do you enjoy working with most?

Age or life stage:

Key concerns or goals:

What are they hoping to feel or experience after a session?

What do you want people to say about your massage practice?

"They really know how to..."

"It just feels so..."

"I trust them because..."

Write a sentence that sums up your *ideal client experience*:

_____

_____

_____

3. Finding Your Voice

Which words best describe the tone you want to strike in your brand?

- ☐ Friendly
- ☐ Reassuring
- ☐ Grounded
- ☐ Direct
- ☐ Quirky
- ☐ Professional
- ☐ Calm
- ☐ Educational
- ☐ Gentle
- ☐ Energetic
- ☐ Honest
- ☐ Warm

Are there any words or tones you *don't* want to use?

_____

Write a few sentences like you would on your website or social media:

Hi, I'm _____. I help people who feel _____ to feel _____ again, using _____.

You're welcome here exactly as you are. Let's get you feeling better.

___

4. Visual Identity (Optional)

Preferred colour palette or inspiration:

___

Any images, textures, or themes that resonate with you (e.g. ocean, forest, anatomy, simplicity):

___

Logo ideas or keywords:

___

___

5. Your Brand in One Line

If you had to sum up your business in a sentence or tagline, what would it be?

"Helping people _____ through _____."

"Gentle, effective massage therapy for _____."

Write yours:

___

Chapter 20: Finding Your Niche and Ideal Client

The people you love to work with are out there—you just need to know how to find them.

When you first qualify as a massage therapist, it can feel like you need to be everything to everyone. You want to help all the people with all the things. And to be fair, there's nothing wrong with being open to a variety of clients—especially when you're still gaining experience.

But over time, something happens. You start noticing who you really love working with.

Is it the stressed-out teacher who visibly melts when they lie down? The weekend runner who lights up when their hips feel freer? Maybe it's the postnatal parent who just needs someone to see them?

That's your niche starting to speak.

Let's explore how to find it—and why doing so can make your practice more fulfilling, sustainable, and successful.

What Is a Niche?

Your niche isn't just a treatment type like "pregnancy massage" or "sports massage."

It's the intersection of:

Who you love working with

What you're good at

What people are looking for (and willing to pay for)

It could be:

A **life stage** (new parents, retirees, teenagers)

A **condition** (chronic pain, stress, fatigue)

A **profession or lifestyle** (dancers, tradespeople, desk workers)

A **community** (LGBTQIA+, neurodivergent, trauma survivors)

A **treatment style** (gentle and nurturing, strong and corrective)

You don't have to limit yourself to just one—but clarity helps people know if you're the right therapist for them.

Why Having a Niche Helps (Even If It Feels Scary)

Therapists often worry that choosing a niche will turn people away. But here's the thing:

When you try to speak to everyone, no one hears you. When you speak directly to the person you most want to reach, they stop scrolling. They lean in. They book.

Some benefits of having a niche:

Easier and more focused marketing

Deeper expertise and confidence

Stronger client loyalty

More referrals (from happy clients and other professionals)

It's also more satisfying. Working with clients you genuinely connect with can protect against burnout and help you feel energised by your work.

How to Find Your Niche

Start by reflecting on these questions:

1. Who do I love working with? (Think about the clients who leave you feeling fulfilled. What do they have in common?)

2. What kinds of problems do I enjoy solving? (Is it helping someone move more freely? Sleep better? Feel emotionally safe?)

3. What do people already come to me for? (Even early on, you'll notice trends in what people ask about.)

4. What lived experiences or backgrounds do I bring to the table? (You might resonate with certain clients because you've walked a similar path. That's powerful.)

5. Is there a group that's underserved in my area? (Sometimes your niche finds you when you notice a gap that needs filling.)

Your Ideal Client

Once you've started to narrow in on your niche, go deeper. Create a little profile in your mind (or on paper):

What is their day like?

What are they struggling with?

What do they want from a massage—not just physically, but emotionally or mentally?

How do they want to feel after seeing you?

The more clearly you can picture this person, the easier it is to speak their language in your marketing, write your website copy, and design services that meet their needs.

A Personal Note

When I first started out, I thought I had to prove I could do everything: sports massage, Relaxation, Trigger points, Pregnancy care, Injury rehab, you name it.

As time went on, I started to notice the difference between clients who inspired me and those who left me feeling drained or unsettled. The shift didn't happen overnight. But when I leaned into the work I truly loved, everything felt easier. Clients started finding me, not the other way around.

Your niche doesn't box you in—it anchors you. It gives you direction, confidence, and a community to serve with heart.

Your niche is where your passion, skills, and client need meet

A clear niche makes marketing easier and your work more rewarding

You can evolve or refine your niche over time—it doesn't have to be forever

Get to know your ideal client like a friend

Don't be afraid to claim your space—it's how the right clients find you

Discovering Your own Niche and Ideal Client

Part 1: Reflection – Who Do You Love Working With?

1. Think about your past sessions (student clinic, case studies, or early clients):

- Which sessions felt energising and satisfying?

- To whom did you feel most connected?

- What made those sessions memorable?

Your thoughts:

---

2. What kind of work do you find yourself naturally drawn to?
(e.g., slow, and nurturing sessions, focused trigger point work, emotional support through touch)

3. Are there any groups or communities you feel especially aligned with or passionate about serving?
(e.g., LGBTQIA+ clients, pregnant clients, carers, FIFO workers, trauma survivors)

4. What strengths, individual experiences, or areas of study make you uniquely suited to support those clients?

Part 2: Clarifying Your Niche

Use the diagram below to brainstorm and narrow in on a niche.

What you love doing:

What you're good at:

What people need and are willing to pay for:

The overlap = Your potential niche

Part 3: Create Your Ideal Client Profile

Imagine your dream client walks through the door. Answer the following questions to get to know them better.

Name (just for fun): _____

Age/life stage: _____

Profession or lifestyle: _____

What stresses or aches do they commonly have?

_____

What do they hope to get out of a massage session—beyond pain relief?

(e.g., emotional reset, better sleep, calmness, movement freedom)

_____

What matters most to them in a therapist?

- ☐ Trust and safety
- ☐ Deep knowledge
- ☐ Nurturing energy
- ☐ Strong hands
- ☐ Clear communication
- ☐ Something else: _____

Where might they be looking for someone like you?

(e.g., social media, health directories, word-of-mouth, gym, local community)

_____

In 1–2 sentences, describe the kind of massage therapist you want to be known as:

"I support _____who are looking for

_____ through massage that feels

_____."

Chapter 21: Building an Online Presence

Helping people find you, trust you, and feel confident enough to book.

When you picture starting your massage practice, you might imagine hands-on sessions, a calm treatment room, or meaningful conversations with clients—not necessarily writing website blurbs or posting on social media. And yet, in today's world, your online presence often becomes the first impression people have of you.

Whether someone finds you through a referral, a local Google search, or a social post that pops up on their feed, chances are they'll look you up online before deciding to book. They're hoping to feel reassured. They want to know they're in the right place, with the right person.

The goal here isn't to become an expert in digital marketing. It's to make your online presence *clear, welcoming, and findable*. Let's walk through how to do that—without the overwhelm.

Be Where You Need to Be (Not Everywhere)

One of the most common misconceptions is that you need to be on *every* platform—website, Facebook, Instagram, TikTok, YouTube and LinkedIn. That's simply not true.

When you're just starting out, it's far more effective (and far less stressful) to choose one or two key places to show up and do those well.

Start with the essentials: a professional booking page or website, and a Google Business Profile.

A simple, clear website—or even just a booking page through a platform like Cliniko, Square, or Fresha—can do a lot of heavy lifting. This is your digital home base, and it should include your location, services, pricing, and how to make an appointment. People shouldn't have to dig around to figure out how to book with you or for what they're booking.

In addition to your booking page, setting up a Google Business Profile is one of the most valuable things you can do. It's free and makes you visible in local searches and on Google Maps. When someone types in "massage near me," you'll have a much better chance of showing up. You can include your business hours, photos, location, contact information, and even gather reviews.

If you feel ready for more visibility, adding just one social media platform—like Facebook or Instagram—can help clients get a feel for your personality, your values, and the kind of experience they might have with you.

Think Like a New Client

If someone lands on your website or profile, what are they seeing? More importantly—what are they *feeling*?

Most new clients are quietly wondering:

- "Is this person professional but also approachable?"
- "Do they seem trustworthy and kind?"
- "Will they understand my situation?"
- "How do I book, and how soon can I get in?"

Your online presence should answer all of those questions gently and clearly.

Start with your tone. The words you use matter. Write the way you speak—warm, human, clear. Avoid jargon and overly clinical language. If your ideal client is a tired parent or someone new to massage, make sure your writing feels reassuring, not intimidating.

Add a friendly photo of yourself, even if you're camera-shy. People connect with faces. It helps them feel more comfortable—and in massage therapy, comfort is everything.

Then think about your service descriptions. Do they reflect what you offer? Are they written in a way that someone with no massage experience could understand? Be specific about who you help, what kind of massage you provide, and what a first appointment might feel like.

If someone lands on your page and instantly feels like you "get" them, they're much more likely to book.

Build Trust Through Consistency

Every piece of your online presence—from your website to your social media to your booking confirmations—tells your client something about your business.

Using the same business name, colour palette, and tone of voice across your platforms builds trust. It creates a sense of coherence. Whether someone finds you through Instagram or a Google listing, they should feel like they're meeting the same person.

It's also important to keep your information up to date. If your hours have changed, if your pricing has increased, or if you're taking a break— make sure that's reflected wherever people might be looking. Outdated details create uncertainty and can lead to lost bookings.

You don't have to have it all perfect right away. This is something you'll refine as you grow. But a few thoughtful updates go a long way in helping people feel confident choosing you.

Social Media: Use It Your Way

Let's talk about social media—because for some therapists, it's a creative joy, and for others, it's a source of stress.

Here's the thing: You do *not* have to post daily. You don't have to make videos, follow trends, or spend your time trying to "go viral."

What matters more is showing up *authentically and sustainably*.

You might post once or twice a week. Share a behind-the-scenes glimpse of your treatment space. Talk about what you love most in your work. Offer a simple self-care tip, a quote that resonates with your values, or an update on your availability.

Let your audience see who you are—not just as a therapist, but as a person who genuinely cares.

You can use scheduling tools (like Later or Meta's own business suite) to plan a few posts ahead and take the pressure off. But remember: your online presence should work *for* you—not the other way around.

Starting Small

I'll never forget setting up my first website. It felt awkward. I overthought every sentence. I wasn't sure what to call my massage style. I worried my photos weren't polished enough.

But do you know what? It still worked.

Clients found me. They resonated with the way I described my work. Some even said, "I booked because your website just felt reassuring." And that's the point. You don't need perfection. You just need honesty, clarity, and a little bit of heart.

Summary

- A solid online presence helps potential clients feel safe, informed, and ready to book

- Start with a professional booking page or website and a Google Business Profile

- Write like a human—use warm, clear, client-friendly language

- Be consistent in your tone, visuals, and business details across platforms

- Use social media in a way that feels manageable and aligned with *you*

- Don't aim for perfection—aim for connection

Your Online Presence Checklist

Website or Booking Page

- I have a website or booking page (via Square, Cliniko, Fresha, etc.)

- My business name, logo (if I have one), and contact info are clearly visible

- I've listed my services in clear, client-friendly language

- My pricing is visible and up to date

- There is a simple, direct way to book (button, link, calendar)

- I've included a short bio or welcome message that feels personal and authentic

- There are photos of my space or me to help new clients feel comfortable

- I've added a "What to Expect" or FAQ section to reduce first-time anxiety

Google Business Profile

- I've claimed my free Google Business listing

- My business address, phone number, and hours are accurate

- I've uploaded a few photos (room, logo, street front, or friendly face)

- I've added a concise description of my services and style

- I've asked at least one happy client for a Google review

- I check and update my listing regularly (especially holidays or changes)

Social Media (Optional but Helpful)

Choose just one platform to begin (e.g. Instagram, Facebook):

- My username and profile photo match my business name

- My bio clearly says what I do and where I'm located

- I've added a booking link or contact method

- I've posted at least 3–6 posts that give a sense of who I am and how I work

- I'm posting in a way that feels manageable (weekly, fortnightly, etc.)

- I use my own voice—personal, professional, and real

- I follow a few local businesses or accounts in my niche to build connection

General Consistency

- My business name and details are the same across all platforms

- My tone and message feel "like me"

- All links work and direct people to the right place

- I update my availability and announcements as needed

Optional Extras

- I've shared a client testimonial (with permission)

- I've written a short blog or posted tips that reflect my niche

- I have a welcome message or video to introduce myself

- I offer a brief explanation of how my massage can help specific issues (e.g. stress, pain, pregnancy)

This is about creating a trustworthy space online that reflects who you are and makes it easy for the right clients to say yes.

Chapter 22: Offline Visibility – Getting Noticed in the Real World

Because not everything has to happen online.

In a world that often feels obsessed with social media metrics and digital marketing hacks, there's something beautifully grounding about building your business the old-fashioned way—through face-to-face conversations, community presence, and good word of mouth.

Offline visibility is about creating a presence in the real world. It's how you let your local community know you're here, you're credible, and you're worth trusting with their health and wellbeing. It's about being memorable in all the quiet, authentic ways that build a sustainable practice over time.

If online visibility invites clients in, offline visibility reminds people that you're part of *their* world—that your hands, your skills, and your care are nearby and ready when they need you.

Let's explore how to do that thoughtfully.

Show Up Where Your Clients Already Are

The best visibility strategy starts by asking, *where are my ideal clients spending their time?*

Are they going to yoga classes or gym sessions? Are they dropping their kids at school? Shopping at the local farmers market? Visiting a nearby physiotherapist? Attending community events?

Start by identifying 2–3 places in your local area where your people already go—then explore how you can gently place yourself in those spaces, not with pressure or sales tactics, but with presence and relevance.

Here are a few ideas to consider:

Build Relationships with Other Professionals

You're not an island. Connecting with other allied health professionals and small business owners can open doors for referrals and collaborations.

- Introduce yourself to nearby physiotherapists, chiropractors, GPs, doulas, or psychologists. Let them know what kind of clients you work best with.

- Offer to exchange business cards or flyers—or just a friendly chat over coffee.

- Consider building a "referral loop" where you support each other with client care.

- Join your local business networking group or allied health association events (even one a quarter can make a significant difference).

These relationships take time to grow, but they build trust—and trust leads to client referrals.

Leave a Physical Presence

It might seem old-school, but thoughtfully designed business cards, postcards, or flyers can still work wonders.

- Place them in places that align with your values: health food shops, Pilates studios, cafes with community boards, or coworking spaces.

- Include a photo or friendly language so people connect more easily.

- Add a simple call-to-action like "Scan to Book" or "Relax Starts Here."

Make sure your print materials reflect your brand. If your niche is gentle, trauma-aware massage, your flyer should feel calm and comforting—not shouty or busy. If your niche is sporty and upbeat, go for bold, clean, and strong.

The Power of Word of Mouth

Word of mouth is still the strongest marketing tool for most massage therapists. It's built on trust, and it keeps working long after the first conversation.

The most effective way to generate positive word of mouth is to give every client an experience they want to talk about: one that feels personal, respectful, and results-driven (even if the result is simply "I finally relaxed!").

That said, you *can* gently encourage word of mouth without being pushy:

- Let regular clients know you're taking on new bookings, and that referrals are welcome.

- Offer a referral card or small thank-you gesture if that suits your style.

- Make sure your clients know exactly what services you offer—sometimes people don't refer because they're not clear!

Host or Attend Local Events

You don't need to be a public speaker to share what you do. Consider:

- Giving a short free talk at your local library, women's centre, gym, or mothers' group

- Donating a voucher to a raffle or fundraiser (good visibility, and community goodwill)

- Hosting a small open house in your treatment space to let people see what you offer

- Attending health or wellbeing expos with a few friends or fellow therapists

Being seen, heard, and part of something local builds familiarity. People are far more likely to book when you feel like someone they've already met.

Make Yourself Easy to Remember

If someone meets you at a market, sees your flyer in a yoga studio, or hears about you through a friend—can they find you easily?

- Keep your business name consistent

- Add your website or booking link on print material

- Have a short, memorable line to describe what you do ("I specialise in gentle, trauma-informed massage for people who don't like deep pressure" is much more effective than "I'm a massage therapist")

- Be proud of what you offer, and don't be afraid to share it when people ask what you do

A Quiet Approach Still Works

You don't need to be loud to be visible. You don't need to be pushy to be booked.

Some of the most successful therapists are booked months in advance because they focused on showing up consistently, being kind, and offering a thoughtful, high-quality service. They didn't flood every market stall or throw business cards at everyone in sight.

They simply showed up in the right places, connected genuinely, and allowed their work to speak for itself.

Remember

- You don't have to be everywhere—just *somewhere meaningful*
- Look for ways to show up where your ideal clients already spend time
- Build gentle referral relationships with other professionals
- Use printed materials in a way that aligns with your brand and energy
- Word of mouth still works—especially when your client experience is memorable
- Local events, talks, or sponsorships help build familiarity and trust
- Be consistent, authentic, and easy to find

Chapter 23: Building Your Reputation and Credibility

Why how you're known matters just as much as what you do.

When you're new to practice, your reputation doesn't arrive fully formed—it grows with you. Every interaction you have, every treatment you give, every message you send contributes to the story people tell about your work.

Reputation isn't about being good at massage (though that helps!). It's about being *dependable. Professional. Real.* It's about the way you show up—when people are watching, and when they're not.

You don't need to be perfect to build a strong reputation. But you do need to be thoughtful, consistent, and committed to your values. Because in this line of work, your reputation *is* your business card.

Let's look at how to build a reputation that feels as solid and warm as the hands you work with.

Be Reliable, First and Always

The fastest way to build (or lose) credibility is reliability. Show up when you say you will. Respond when you promise to. Follow through on the little things, like sending a confirmation message or having your room ready on time.

You don't have to bend over backward to be accommodating—but being dependable creates a sense of trust that's hard to beat.

Things that quietly build trust:

Starting and finishing sessions on time

Communicating clearly and kindly if you're running late or need to reschedule

Honouring client boundaries, time, and preferences

Maintaining accurate records

Staying consistent in your policies, pricing, and communication

These small actions say, "You can count on me." And that's what people remember.

Ask for (and respond to) Feedback

You don't have to wait ten years to know how you're doing. Asking for feedback—formally or informally—helps you improve, but it also shows that you care.

You might:

Ask a new client how they felt after the session

Include a follow-up message 24–48 hours later with space for comments

Send a brief survey after the first three months of business

Invite Google reviews with a simple, friendly message

If you receive positive feedback, thank the client and celebrate that moment. If you receive something more constructive, take a breath, take it seriously, and see what you can learn.

Responding to feedback with humility and care builds your reputation faster than any ad campaign ever could.

Be Consistent (Even When No One's Watching)

Professionalism isn't about putting on a show when clients are around—it's about keeping your standards steady, whether it's a new client or your best regular.

Do you clean the room between each session even when your next client's a friend? Do you maintain your paperwork even when you're tired? Do you communicate respectfully even when something goes wrong?

Reputation is built in those quiet choices. You don't have to get everything right—but your clients will notice when you care enough to be consistent.

Gather and Share Testimonials (With Permission)

Social proof matters, especially in an industry built on trust. A kind word from someone who's experienced your work can go a long way.

Here's how to approach it:

Ask regular clients if they'd be happy to provide a testimonial

Let them write it in their own words (authenticity matters more than polish)

With permission, use those words on your website, booking platform, or socials

Always respect their privacy and offer the option to stay anonymous or use first names only

You can even create a little "Client Love" section on your site or print out a couple of kind words and frame them in your clinic. You're not showing off—you're offering reassurance to the next person who might really need your care.

Back It Up With Your Online Presence

If your online presence doesn't match the professional, warm experience of your real-life practice, it can create doubt.

Your website and socials don't have to be perfect, but they should reflect:

Who you are

What you offer

What it feels like to work with you

Update your info regularly. Make it easy to book. Make it easy to understand. When your online and offline reputations match, your credibility multiplies.

Be Kind. It Sticks.

Your skill matters, but your *energy* stays with people long after they leave the room.

Be kind when someone's nervous. Be patient when someone's confused. Be generous with your knowledge when it's helpful. And be willing to say, "I'm not sure—but I'll find out."

Kindness doesn't mean you have no boundaries—it means your professionalism is wrapped in care. And that is what builds a reputation that lasts.

Chapter 24: Content That Connects

How to share your message in a way that feels authentic—and resonates.

Marketing can be one of the hardest parts of building a massage practice—not because you're not good at what you do, but because it feels unnatural to talk about it.

We often imagine content has to be polished, persuasive, even a bit pushy. But the truth is, the most effective content is just *you*, speaking clearly to the people who need your work the most.

Whether you're writing a social media caption, updating your website, or creating a handout for clients, your content doesn't need to be flashy. It just needs to be *real*. Helpful. Relevant. Reassuring.

In this chapter, we'll explore how to create content that doesn't just fill space—but connects with the people you're here to serve.

What Does "Content" Mean?

When we say "content," we're talking about anything you create or share to communicate your work with others.

That might include:

- Website text or blog posts

- Social media posts

- Email newsletters

- Printed handouts or brochures

- Booking page descriptions

- Welcome packs

- Posters or flyers

- Video introductions

- Client resources and guides

Anything that helps people understand *what you offer* and *why it matters*—that's content.

Speak Like a Human, Not a Billboard

A lot of new therapists fall into the trap of trying to sound "professional" at the expense of sounding like themselves. You don't need corporate jargon or over-polished wording. You just need clarity, warmth, and authenticity.

Instead of:

"Our clinic utilises evidence-based techniques to support holistic wellbeing."

Try something like:

"I help people feel better in their bodies using a mix of remedial massage, gentle movement, and supportive care."

Speak like you would to a curious friend. Explain your services the way you'd explain them to someone who's never had a massage before. That's what makes people feel safe and seen.

Know Who You're Talking To

Useful content doesn't try to speak to *everyone*. It's written with a particular kind of person in mind—your *ideal client*.

Ask yourself:

- What's this person going through?

- What do they care about?

- What would make them feel understood?

- What questions or hesitations might they have?

Then, shape your content around those answers.

For example, if your niche is working with people living with chronic pain, your content might include gentle reassurance, realistic expectations, and small wins—rather than bold promises or fast results.

Reassurance Over Persuasion

Your job isn't to "convince" someone to book. It's to *reassure* the right person that they're in the right place.

That might sound like:

- "If you've been living with tension for years, and you're not sure massage will help—you're not alone. I work gently and patiently, and we can take it one step at a time."

- "I offer quiet, unhurried sessions for people who want a break from the rush."

- "You don't have to be in pain to benefit from massage. Many of my clients just want to feel a little more at ease in their body."

This kind of content makes people feel safe—and that's the real secret to booking solid clients.

Make It Useful

Helpful content builds trust.

You could:

- Post a simple breathing exercise for stress

- Share tips on preparing for a first massage

- Write a short article on how massage can help with headaches or posture

- Create a handout about aftercare (what to expect after a session)

- Record a video answering the question, "Do I have to be in pain to benefit from remedial massage?"

When people find your content useful—even before they book—you become someone they turn to for guidance. That's connection.

Plan It, Don't Panic It

You don't need to post every day or update your blog weekly. But having a simple plan helps you stay consistent without burning out.

Start small:

- One social post a week

- One new page or update on your website each season

- One email every month or two to check in with your clients

You can even recycle your content—share the same ideas in different ways. A blog post becomes a social post. A client handout becomes a website update. Keep it simple and sustainable.

Examples of Content That Connects

Here are a few real-world ideas to spark inspiration:

- **"A day in the life"** post showing your setup routine before clients arrive

- **Welcome message** on your booking page: "Hi, I'm Amy. I help tired, overworked humans feel a little more human again."

- **Educational reel or story**: "3 Things to Know Before Your First Massage"

- **Reflection post**: "What I've learned from 6 months of working with new mums"

- **Client win** (with permission): "Sarah came in with constant shoulder tension. After a few sessions, she said she finally slept through the night."

Don't Be Afraid to Be You

Some people will really appreciate your calm, steady way of being. Others will be drawn to your energy and strength. You don't have to tone yourself down for anyone. Just show up as you really are. That's what people connect with. And when they feel that connection, they're more likely to trust you to take care of them.

Write Your Bio – Cheat Sheet

An uncomplicated guide to writing a bio that sounds like you (and helps the right clients find you).

Step 1: Start with a Warm Hello

Open with something friendly and personal. You don't have to launch into credentials right away. Imagine introducing yourself to someone at a community event.

Prompt:

"Hi, I'm [your name], and I help…"
"I'm a [your title], passionate about…"
"You'll usually find me…"

Examples:

"Hi, I'm Nina. I help people unwind and reconnect with their bodies through thoughtful, personalised massage."
"I'm a remedial massage therapist based in Adelaide, and I love working with people who carry a lot—physically or emotionally."

Step 2: Explain What You Do

Let people know what kind of massage you offer, and who you love working with. Be clear and kind—jargon isn't necessary.

Prompt:

"My sessions focus on..."
"I work with clients who..."
"Whether you're experiencing [common issues] or just need..."

Examples:

"I work with people experiencing chronic tension, anxiety, or burnout. My treatments are gentle, effective, and always tailored to your needs."
"Whether you're recovering from injury, training for an event, or need a break from your busy week—I've got you."

Step 3: Share What Makes You Unique

Add a distinctive touch. What's your approach, vibe, or philosophy? What do clients often say about working with you?

Prompt:

"Clients often tell me..."
"I believe massage should..."
"My approach is..."

Examples:

"Clients often tell me they feel safe, supported, and deeply relaxed after our sessions."
"My approach is slow, steady, and respectful—ideal for people who don't love deep pressure but still want lasting relief."

Step 4: Add Any Optional Details

You can include your qualifications, location, or how long you've been practising here—but keep it natural and relevant.

Prompt:

"I'm a qualified [modality] therapist, with additional training in..."
"I work from a peaceful space in..."
"Before massage, I worked in..."

Examples:

"I'm a qualified remedial massage therapist, with additional training in oncology massage and trauma-aware care."
"My clinic is in the heart of Port Adelaide, just above the yoga studio."

Step 5: Invitation to Book

Finish with a gentle invitation. No need for salesy language—just a clear next step.

Prompt:

"You're welcome to book online or reach out with questions."
"If this sounds like the kind of care you need, I'd love to work with you."

Example:

"If you're looking for thoughtful, down-to-earth massage that puts your needs first—you're in the right place. You can book online or send me a message with any questions."

Final Checklist

☑ Is your tone warm and conversational?

☑ Does it sound like you?

☑ Can someone quickly understand who you work with and what you offer?

☑ Did you avoid too much jargon?

☑ Did you include a clear way to book or get in touch?

Part Five: Ethics, Boundaries, and Communication

Chapter 25: Understanding Boundaries

Holding Space without losing Yourself

When we talk about boundaries in massage therapy, people often assume we're just talking about client behaviour—what's allowed, what isn't, how to manage awkward situations. And yes, that's part of it. But true professional boundaries go deeper.

Boundaries aren't just rules—they're relationships. They shape the way we work, the energy we bring into the room, the expectations we hold for ourselves and our clients. And perhaps most importantly, they keep us *whole*. They help us show up fully present, without being pulled into roles that don't serve us.

Many therapists—especially those who are new or highly empathetic—struggle with boundaries. We want to help. We want to give. We want to make things easier for people. And sometimes, we forget that *we* matter too.

This chapter is about learning to hold your space gently but firmly. It's not about building walls—it's about setting down foundations so you can care without collapsing, give without losing, and work sustainably, with love and clarity.

What Are Boundaries?

Boundaries are the lines we draw—consciously or not—around our time, our energy, our emotional availability, and our professional role. They help define:

What you're responsible for (and what you're not)

How clients can contact you (and when)

What happens in a session (and what doesn't)

How you protect your space, your energy, and your values

Think of boundaries as your practice's nervous system. You don't always see it, but it helps everything run smoothly.

Why Boundaries Can Be Hard

If you've ever felt awkward about saying no, found yourself over-giving in sessions, or dreaded replying to a client's 10pm message—you're not alone.

We're often taught that good practitioners are endlessly giving, flexible, available, and self-sacrificing. But that mindset doesn't serve anyone. Not you, not your clients.

Healthy boundaries aren't about being rigid—they're about being clear.

Boundaries in Action

Let's bring this down to earth. Here are a few ways boundaries show up in daily practice:

Booking and Availability

You set your hours. You decide when (and if) you answer messages. If someone texts asking for a last-minute Sunday night appointment and you're not available—you don't owe them an apology. You owe yourself rest.

Communication

A client sends multiple messages outside business hours. A boundary could look like setting an autoreply or kindly explaining that you check messages during set times.

"Thanks so much for your message! I'll get back to you during my admin hours on Monday."

Scope of Practice

A client asks for advice that steps outside your professional boundaries—something medical or psychological. It's okay (and necessary) to say:

"That's a bit outside my scope, but I can refer you to someone who specialises in that area."

Energy and Emotional Load

Some clients come with big stories. You can hold space without absorbing it. You're not a counsellor (unless you are!). It's okay to gently redirect, to pause, or to take a breath.

"That sounds hard. If you ever want to talk more about that, a counsellor could be a great support. In the meantime, let's help your body feel more at ease today."

Setting Boundaries Before You Need Them

One of the kindest things you can do for your future self is to plan your boundaries *in advance*. That way, when something tricky pops up (and it will), you're not scrambling to figure it out mid-crisis.

Some things to consider:

What hours do I want to work?

How will I handle late cancellations or no-shows?

How will clients contact me—and what are my response times?

What am I willing and unwilling to do in a session?

What kind of clients or cases might I choose to refer out?

Write these down. They can form the basis for your policies, welcome packs, and even how you talk about your practice online.

Boundaries = Care

Boundaries aren't about pushing people away. They're about creating a space where trust, safety, and respect can flourish.

When clients know where the lines are, they feel *held*. When *you* know where the lines are, you feel *grounded*. It's not a power struggle—it's a partnership.

Remember: boundaries don't make you less caring. They make your care more sustainable.

Boundary Self-Check Planner

A gentle pause to check in with how you're holding space for yourself.

Boundaries don't need to be perfect—but they *do* need to be practiced.

Use this short self-check to reflect on where your boundaries are holding strong, where they're feeling a little wobbly, and where you might want to make small shifts.

You can revisit this any time—especially when things feel heavy or unclear.

Communication

Do I feel comfortable with how clients contact me?

☐ Yes

☐ Mostly

☐ Not really

Do I check and reply to messages on a schedule that works for me?

☐ Yes

☐ Sometimes

☐ I often feel rushed or guilty

Note to self: What's one small boundary I could set or reinforce around client communication?

Time & Availability

Am I working within the hours that suit my body, lifestyle, and energy?

☐ Yes

☐ Mostly

☐ I often overbook or overextend

Do I take breaks, lunch, and days off regularly?

☐ Yes

☐ Sometimes

☐ I feel guilty or fall behind

Note to self: What's one way I could protect my time more gently but clearly?

Emotional Energy

Do I leave sessions feeling grounded more often than drained?

☐ Yes

☐   It varies

☐   I often feel depleted

Can I hold space for clients without taking their emotions home with me?

☐   Yes

☐   I try, but it's hard

☐   I often carry it around

Note to self: What helps me release energy after a session? What boundary might help?

Scope of Practice

Do I feel confident redirecting or referring when something is outside my role?

☐   Yes

☐   I sometimes hesitate

☐   I often blur the lines or feel unsure

Do I clearly communicate what I *do* and *don't* offer?

☐   Yes

☐   Sort of

☐   Not clearly

Note to self: Where might I need more clarity—for myself or for clients?

Overall

How do my boundaries feel right now?

☐   Strong and supportive

☐   Okay, but needs refinement

☐   Pretty blurry or too harsh

If my future self could thank me for one minor change, what would it be?

Write a sentence or two here.

_____

_____

_____

_____

Boundaries are essential for sustainability and professionalism.

They protect your energy, time, and role as a therapist.

Planning your boundaries in advance gives you confidence and clarity.

Boundaries can be communicated kindly—they're not mean, they're necessary.

Healthy boundaries create safer, more respectful spaces for everyone.

Chapter 26: Consent and Client Communication

Clarity, kindness, and keeping the client in charge of their body.

Massage therapists often talk about consent, but in practice, it's easy to default to routine. We ask if the pressure is okay, or if the client is comfortable—but true, ongoing, informed consent is about much more than that.

Consent is about *collaboration.* It's a shared understanding between you and the person on your table. It's a way of saying:

"You're the expert on your body. I'm here to help—but you're in control."

When consent becomes part of your everyday language, your clients feel safer, more respected, and more empowered. It builds trust. It strengthens your reputation. And honestly? It just feels better—for both of you.

What Consent Actually Means

Consent isn't just about saying "yes" or "no" at the start of a session. It's a process—not a checkbox.

To be meaningful, consent should always be:

Informed – The client knows exactly what to expect

Voluntary – They're choosing freely, without pressure

Ongoing – It can change or be withdrawn at any time

Specific – It applies to each part of the treatment, not just the whole

Before the Session: Setting the Tone

This starts the moment someone books in.

Use your welcome email or confirmation message to explain what they can expect. This might include things like:

What to wear or bring

Whether they'll need to fill in an intake form

How long the session goes for

A reminder that they're always in control and can ask questions

During the first appointment, take time to go over the treatment plan. Say something like:

"Here's what I'm thinking for today. I'll start with your upper back and shoulders, using gentle pressure to start. Let me know how that feels—we can adjust anything."

You're not just asking permission. You're creating *collaborative care*.

During the Session: Checking In Regularly

Some clients will speak up easily. Others won't. That's why it helps to check in occasionally—with warmth, not worry.

Try phrases like:

"How's the pressure here?"

"Would you like me to avoid that area today?"

"Is it okay if I move on to your glutes next?"

"If anything feels uncomfortable at all, just let me know and I'll adjust right away."

You don't need to interrupt the session constantly—but a few well-placed check-ins go a long way.

Tip: Clients who are trauma-affected, neurodivergent, or anxious might not *say* anything when they're uncomfortable. Sometimes "everything's fine" means "I'm trying to tolerate this."

That's why your tone matters just as much as your words.

After the Session: Inviting Feedback

Aftercare is part of consent too. Invite honest feedback, even if it's awkward. That way, your client knows their voice matters.

You might say:

"How are you feeling after the session?"

"Was there anything you'd like different next time—more or less pressure, different areas, anything at all?"

"This is a learning process for me too—your feedback helps me improve."

If something *does* go wrong—a miscommunication, a client feels uncomfortable, or there's a misunderstanding—it's okay to acknowledge it. Listen without defensiveness. Respond with care.

What About Complex or Grey Areas?

Sometimes, you'll run into consent challenges that don't have a clear script.

A client insists on something outside your scope.

"Thanks for trusting me with that. I want to make sure you're properly supported—this is outside my training, but I can refer you to someone who specialises in it."

You're treating someone who struggles with body awareness or decision fatigue.

Go slower. Break things down. Offer choices. Use phrases like:

"Here are a couple of options—would either of those be okay?"

You suspect the client is agreeing out of politeness.

Normalize changing their mind:

"Just a reminder—this is your session. We can stop, pause, or change things at any time."

Building Consent Into Your Systems

Your paperwork can support your consent process. Intake forms, privacy statements, and treatment plans should all reinforce:

- What kind of treatment you offer
- What clients can expect
- Their right to stop, modify, or decline anything
- How their information is stored and used

These documents aren't just for protection—they're part of creating a respectful, transparent relationship.

When in Doubt: Ask, Don't Assume

Even if a client has seen you a dozen times, don't assume their needs haven't changed. Some days people want quiet. Some days they want to talk. Some days their body feels different, and so does their capacity for touch.

Asking is respectful. Adjusting is powerful.

And listening? That's your greatest skill.

Bringing Consent to Life

Consent isn't just a formality—it's a living, breathing part of every client interaction. It starts with clear, respectful communication before the session and continues throughout, with gentle check-ins and an openness to change course if needed. As therapists, we can foster trust by making consent part of our everyday language—using warm, non-clinical phrases and offering real choices without pressure. It's not about ticking boxes, but about building relationships where clients feel seen, heard, and safe. Whether you're creating paperwork, writing policies, or simply greeting someone at the door, let your commitment to client autonomy be felt in every part of your practice.

Chapter 27: Ethics in Practice

Doing the right thing, even when no one's watching

Ethics might sound like a dry or formal topic—but it's deeply personal. It's not just about codes and complaints; it's about how you show up in the world as a therapist and a human being. It's about trust, respect, integrity, and the quiet choices we make every day when no one's supervising, no one's grading, and no one's watching over our shoulder.

When you start practicing independently—whether you're setting up your own business, working in a clinic, or contracting—ethical decision-making becomes entirely your responsibility. And that can feel both empowering and a little daunting. The truth is, there won't always be a black-and-white answer. There will be grey areas, hard calls, and moments that ask you to pause and check in with your values.

In this chapter, we'll explore what ethics looks like in massage therapy—not just in theory, but in real, practical, human terms.

What Is Ethics, Really?

Ethics is about more than simply avoiding wrongdoing. It's the foundation of professional integrity. Ethical practice builds trust—without it, everything falls apart.

In massage therapy, ethical conduct usually centres around:

- Respect for client autonomy

- Privacy and confidentiality

- Informed consent

- Yours and your Client's safety

- Professional boundaries

- Honesty in marketing and claims

- Working within your scope of practice

- Transparency about fees, availability, and qualifications

Each of these areas comes with questions you'll need to revisit repeatedly—especially as you grow and your practice evolves.

Codes of Conduct

In Australia, professional associations such as Massage & Myotherapy Australia or the Association of Massage Therapists provide detailed codes of ethics that outline expectations around client care, documentation, boundaries, advertising, continuing education, and more.

These codes are not just legal protection—they're your compass. They give you a starting point when something feels unclear or uncomfortable.

Even if you're not yet a member of an association, it's worth reading a code of conduct to start shaping your own internal ethical framework. Because eventually, you'll be faced with an ethical choice that won't be covered by a rule book—and your integrity will have to carry the weight.

Common Ethical Dilemmas

Let's look at some of the real-life grey areas that massage therapists often face:

A client discloses something deeply personal—do you keep it private?

Yes, unless it involves risk of harm to themselves or others. Confidentiality is sacred—but there are limits. Know your reporting obligations and have a referral pathway ready.

A client asks for a treatment that you don't feel qualified to offer— what do you say?

Be honest and kind. "That's not something I'm trained in, but I can refer you to someone who specialises in that area." Stretching beyond your skillset might feel helpful in the moment—but it's a slippery slope.

A friend wants a discount, or your aunt wants a free massage "just this once."

Boundaries aren't unethical—but *unequal* treatment can be. If you offer friends and family discounts, have a consistent policy. Transparency is your best friend here.

You want to promote your practice online—how far is too far?

Stick to claims that are evidence-based and within your scope. Avoid language that guarantees outcomes or mimics medical treatments unless you're trained in them. Share what you *do*, not what you *promise*.

Ethics and Self-Awareness

Some of the most powerful ethical tools are internal:

- **Reflection** – Pause and ask, "What sits well with you here?"

- **Supervision or mentoring** – When in doubt, talk it out. Always taking client confidentiality into consideration, of course.

- **Growth mindset** – Ethical clarity often grows with experience. It's okay to not know everything right away.

If something feels off, it probably is. If you're justifying something to yourself, slow down and ask why. Ethics lives in those quiet moments of honesty.

Respecting Client Autonomy

Your clients are not passive recipients of your care—they're participants. That means ethical practice includes:

- Getting informed consent for every treatment or change in plan

- Respecting their right to decline or modify any part of the session

- Empowering them to give feedback without fear or awkwardness

It's not about perfection. It's about partnership.

Ethics in Communication and Marketing

Every message you send—on your website, social media, brochures, and emails—reflects your professional ethics.

Ask yourself:

- Is this honest?

- Is it respectful?

- Am I being clear about what I offer and what I don't?

Never underestimate the power of simple, transparent language. You don't need grand claims—you just need to be real.

Ethics in Your Inner World

What about the ethical obligation to yourself?

You are part of the picture too. Ethical practice includes treating yourself with dignity—setting boundaries, honouring your limits, investing in ongoing education, and avoiding burnout and exploitation. A depleted therapist can't offer safe, ethical care.

Ask:

- Am I treating myself as respectfully as I treat my clients?

- Am I staying in integrity with my own needs and energy?

Reflection

Ethics is not a one-time conversation or a list of rules on a wall. It's an ongoing practice—a way of showing up with intention, humility, and humanity.

You will make mistakes. You'll miss things. We all do. But ethical practice isn't about being perfect. It's about being accountable. It's about caring enough to course correct.

You became a massage therapist because you want to help people. Ethical practice is what lets you do that well, and sustainably, for the long term.

Chapter 28: Professional Presentation & Conduct

How you show up matters—before you even speak a word.

When we think of being a great massage therapist, we often focus on technique. And yes, your hands, knowledge, and clinical judgment matter. But *how* you present yourself—your appearance, your tone, your space, and your energy—can set the tone for every client interaction before the treatment even begins.

Your professional presentation isn't about wearing fancy clothes or having a perfect studio. It's about creating safety, trust, and a sense of care. It's about showing respect for the client and for yourself. It's the nonverbal language of professionalism—and it speaks loudly.

Hygiene: Respect in Action

Hygiene isn't just about cleanliness—it's about how your client feels in your presence. It tells them, *you matter. Your health matters. This space is safe for you.*

- **Hands:** Always freshly washed, nails short and clean. Even if you use gloves, this matters.

- **Clothing:** Fresh, appropriate, and comfortable. Nothing too revealing, too casual, or too worn out. Even if you're working from home, your attire should reflect care.

- **Hair & Breath:** Hair pulled back if needed, breath fresh, perfumes kept minimal or avoided altogether.

- **Linen & Space:** Every surface your client touches should be clean. Change linen between clients, wipe down surfaces, and never reuse disposable face cradle covers.

These small habits aren't optional—they're foundational to ethical, respectful care.

Dress the Part—But Make It *You*

You don't need to wear a uniform (unless your clinic asks for it). But what you wear should reflect that you take your work seriously. Consider:

- Comfortable but tidy activewear or scrub-style pants and a plain top

- Branded shirts if you've created a logo or business identity

- Footwear that's clean and quiet (squeaky shoes are surprisingly distracting)

You can still express your personality—just think about how that expression supports your professional identity. Clients should feel confident in you from the moment they see you.

Language & Tone: You're a Professional, Not a Guru

What you say—and how you say it—carries weight.

- Avoid overpromising or making unverified health claims. Say, *"This technique often helps with..."* instead of *"This will fix your..."*

- Don't diagnose. You can describe observations (e.g. "there's some tightness here") but stay within your scope.

- Be careful with casual banter. Friendly is great; overly familiar can feel unprofessional or even unsafe.

- Speak clearly, respectfully, and with confidence. It's okay to say, *"I'm not sure about that, but I can find out."*

Remember, people may be coming to you at their most vulnerable—emotionally, physically, or psychologically. How you speak can either reinforce safety or erode it.

Boundaries Start with Presence

You don't need to become someone else to be professional. In fact, authenticity is one of your greatest assets. But your *presence* matters.

That means:

- Being grounded, calm, and focused when the client arrives

- Not rushing or multitasking while they're trying to explain something

- Greeting them with warmth, not distraction

- Finishing the session with clarity and care—not dashing out the door or going overtime without checking in

Presence is what makes people feel like they're in good hands—even before you've laid a hand on them.

Your Space Is Part of Your Presentation

Even if you're renting a room, working from home, or going mobile, your space speaks volumes.

- **Tidy, uncluttered, and welcoming**. People should feel at ease the moment they walk in

- **Accessible and inclusive**. Consider mobility needs, sensory sensitivities, and diverse body types

- **Smell and sound**. Be mindful of overpowering scents or noisy surroundings

- **Extras like tissues, water, or a small waiting area**. These little touches go a long way

You don't need a luxury spa—but you *do* need to offer a sense of intentional care.

What Undermines Professionalism?

Sometimes it's not the big things—it's the small slip-ups that slowly chip away at trust.

- Being late or running over time without apology

- Forgetting client names or details they've already shared

- Gossiping about other clients or therapists

- Texting or checking your phone during sessions

- Posting unprofessional or inappropriate content online

None of us are perfect—but self-awareness is part of the job. If you mess up, own it, and learn from it. That *is* professionalism in action.

Professionalism Isn't About Pretending

You don't need to hide your personality, become robotic, or sound like a script. In fact, clients appreciate your humanness. But professional presentation is about showing that *you respect yourself, your client, and the work you do.*

It's about *trust.* And that trust starts the moment your client walks through the door—or even before.

The Small Things That Say a Lot

Professional presentation isn't about looking fancy or being perfect—it's about care, consistency, and clarity. It's the little things you do each day that tell your clients, *"You matter. I'm prepared. You're safe here."*

You don't need to wear a suit or speak like a textbook. You just need to show up in a way that reflects the respect you have for your clients, your profession, and yourself.

That might mean a freshly made table, a warm smile, a clean shirt, and a few deep breaths before you open the door. It might mean catching yourself when you're tempted to rush or pausing before you post something online.

These small choices speak volumes. And over time, they build the kind of reputation that keeps people coming back—not just because of your technique, but because of how you made them feel.

Professionalism, at its heart, is presence. And presence is powerful.

Chapter 29: Confidentiality, Feedback & Complaints

Trust isn't just given—it's earned, protected, and nurtured.

There's a quiet power in the work we do as massage therapists. Clients entrust us with their bodies, their time, and often, parts of their personal story. That trust is sacred—and it's our responsibility to honour it with integrity, professionalism, and empathy.

This chapter explores three pillars of that trust: **confidentiality**, **feedback**, and **complaints**. Each one, in its own way, plays a role in how safe and respected a client feels—and in how sustainable and ethical your practice becomes.

Confidentiality: What's Shared in the Room, Stays in the Room

Confidentiality isn't just a policy—it's a foundation of therapeutic trust. When a client tells you something personal, even in passing, they're trusting you to hold that information with care.

This includes:

- **Health information** from intake forms or verbal disclosures

- **Life circumstances** (e.g., pregnancy, grief, trauma, financial hardship)

- **Treatment notes**, progress updates, or clinical observations

- **Anything overheard** if you work in a shared space or reception area

Even casually sharing stories (anonymised or not) on social media, in peer groups, or with friends can breach confidentiality if you're not careful.

The golden rule? If it's not *your* story, don't tell it.

Confidentiality extends beyond what's said. It includes how you **store client records**, how you **secure booking systems**, and how you

handle client communication (especially if others might access your phone or emails).

Protecting Client Information

Here's how to ensure your records and communication stay secure:

- Use password-protected booking and notes software

- Keep paper files in a locked cabinet (not just in your tote bag)

- Never leave client notes lying out where others can see them

- Don't email sensitive health information unless it's encrypted

- Get consent before sharing any info—even with other practitioners

And if you ever make a mistake or realise something's been compromised? Own it. Apologise. Seek guidance from your association or insurance. Transparency is key.

Encouraging Feedback Without Fear

A thriving practice is one that *welcomes* feedback—not just praise, but the tricky stuff too.

Most clients won't tell you if something feels off. They'll simply stop coming. Creating a culture where feedback is safe, invited, and respected can help you grow as a practitioner *and* keep clients coming back.

You might say at the end of a session:

"If you ever have any feedback—positive or otherwise—I genuinely welcome it. I want to make sure this feels right for you."

You can also:

- Include a feedback question in follow-up emails

- Offer an anonymous feedback form in your welcome pack

- Ask gently during the session: *"Is the pressure okay?"* or *"Would you like more support under your knees?"*

Don't take feedback personally. Think of it as a conversation that helps you fine-tune your care.

What About Complaints?

At some point in your career, you'll receive a complaint. It's never fun— but it's also not the end of the world.

Complaints often arise from:

- Misunderstandings about expectations

- Communication breakdowns

- Accidental oversights

- Clients feeling unheard, rushed, or disrespected

When a complaint arises:

1. **Pause and listen.** Let them speak without interrupting or defending.

2. **Acknowledge.** You can say, *"I'm sorry that happened. I hear that it didn't feel good for you."*

3. **Clarify and respond.** If you need time to think or investigate, let them know.

4. **Reflect and repair.** Use it as a learning opportunity—even if you don't fully agree with the complaint.

And remember, your **professional association** is there to help. Many have clear complaint-handling processes and offer guidance or support if needed.

Boundaries Around Confidentiality & Complaints

There are a few situations where **confidentiality has limits**. These include:

- If a client discloses something that suggests they or someone else is in immediate danger

- If subpoenaed by law

- If you work in a multi-practitioner setting where clinical handover is needed (but only with consent)

In these cases, it's important to know your obligations, get guidance, and document everything clearly.

Real Talk: That Time I Didn't Know What to Say

I'll never forget when a client opened up during a session about their partner's sudden death. I was fresh into practice, and all I could think was: *What do I do now?*

I froze. I didn't want to say the wrong thing. But I also didn't want to ignore it.

I gently asked, *"Would you like to keep talking, or would you like some quiet time?"*

That moment taught me that I don't have to have all the answers. I just have to *be there*—respectfully, calmly, and with a commitment to holding space safely.

Earning—and Keeping—Trust

Your skill as a therapist doesn't end with your hands. It's in how you listen. It's in how you respond when something goes wrong. It's in how you protect what's shared with you, even when no one's watching.

Confidentiality, feedback, and complaints aren't just administrative topics. They're at the heart of professional care.

They help you build a practice that's not only effective—but truly trustworthy.

Chapter 30: Adapting to Client Diversity

Everyone is welcome. Every story matters.

As massage therapists, we work with people—not just bodies. And people bring their whole selves to your table: their history, their identities, their needs, their vulnerabilities. Our job is not just to provide a treatment—it's to create a space where clients feel genuinely seen, safe, and respected.

This chapter is all about learning how to adapt your practice to meet the diverse needs of the people who come through your door. That includes cultural backgrounds, gender identities, body types, neurodiversity, trauma histories, disabilities, and more.

You don't have to be an expert in everything. But you do have to be open, curious, and willing to learn.

Cultural Sensitivity: Understanding Isn't Optional

Culture shapes how people view health, bodies, pain, privacy, gender roles, and even touch. What feels normal or nurturing to you might feel intrusive or inappropriate to someone else.

It's okay if you don't know everything—what matters is how you respond. Instead of making assumptions, try saying:

"Would you prefer a female or male therapist?"

"Are there any areas you'd like me to avoid?"

"Do you have any cultural or personal preferences I should be aware of today?"

And importantly: **never fake cultural fluency.** If you're not sure, it's okay to ask respectfully or seek out resources to learn more. This builds trust and shows clients that you care.

Neurodivergence and Sensory Awareness

Some clients may be autistic, ADHD, or have other forms of neurodivergence—and may or may not disclose this.

Neurodivergent clients might prefer:

- Clear, structured explanations of what will happen during the session

- Advance notice before transitions or changes in routine

- Options for dimmed lights, less noise, or reduced scent

- Permission to wear headphones or stim during intake or treatment

- Control over pressure, positioning, or time limits

Don't assume someone is being "difficult" if they need things a bit different. Meet them where they are.

"Let me know if there's anything I can adjust to make this space more comfortable for you."

This is not only trauma-aware—it's *client-aware*.

Size Inclusion and Body Neutrality

Clients come in all shapes, sizes, and levels of mobility. Your space and your attitude should be prepared for that.

- Have a table that accommodates larger bodies safely and comfortably

- Avoid weight-based comments, even if meant kindly (e.g. "You're doing great with your fitness!")

- Use linens, bolsters, and supports that can adjust for different needs

- Respect clothing choices—some clients may prefer to stay partially clothed, even during massage

- Promote your services using inclusive language and images, not just slim, models without disability

Offer bodywork without judgment. Your job is not to "fix" a body. It's to support it.

Gender and LGBTQIA+ Affirming Practice

It's essential that every client feels safe, regardless of gender identity or sexual orientation.

- Use the name and pronouns your client uses—every time

- Don't assume gender from a name or body

- Have intake forms that are inclusive (e.g., offer non-binary/gender-diverse options)

- Avoid overly gendered language like "ladies" or "mums" unless it's contextually correct and affirming

- Be aware of physical touch areas that may have specific meaning or discomfort for some clients

"Let me know if there's anywhere you'd like me to avoid or if you have any preferences around draping or positioning."

Even if you've never had a client disclose their gender identity or sexuality to you—it matters that your space is affirming by default.

Trauma Awareness Is Everyone's Responsibility

Many clients arrive at your table with invisible stories. They may have experienced:

- Medical trauma

- Sexual assault

- Domestic violence

- Grief and loss

- Chronic illness or marginalisation

You don't need to know the details to practise with care. Trauma-aware practice means:

- Always asking for consent, not assuming it

- Giving clients the option to say "no" or take a break

- Watching for nonverbal cues of discomfort

- Normalising client control: "Would you like to stop here or continue?"

- Staying regulated yourself—your calmness is part of their safety

A trauma-aware therapist knows they are not there to *heal trauma* but to avoid doing further harm.

Accessibility and Inclusion

Is your practice truly accessible?

- Can clients in wheelchairs enter your clinic easily?

- Do you offer mobile options for those who can't travel?

- Are your online booking and forms accessible to screen readers?

- Do you have low-scent or sensory-reduced sessions for those with sensitivities?

- Can someone with limited English or literacy still access your care?

Inclusion is not just about who comes—it's also about who *can't*.

Inclusion Is an Ongoing Practice

You will make mistakes. We all do. What matters is how you respond.

- Apologise if you get it wrong. Then adjust.
- Ask for feedback.
- Update your forms, signage, website, and language.
- Take CPD courses on cultural safety, LGBTQIA+ inclusion, disability awareness, trauma-informed care.
- Be willing to listen, unlearn, and grow.

The goal isn't perfection—it's presence. It's humility. It's creating a space where clients feel like they belong.

A Note from the Heart

One of my most memorable clients told me, "I've never felt comfortable in a massage space before—but you made it feel okay to be myself."

That still makes me emotional.

Because that's what we do—it's so much more than muscle release. We offer people a space where they don't have to hide or shrink or explain.

Part Six: Sustainability and Growth

Chapter 31: Planning for Time Off and Work-Life Balance

You are not a machine. You are a human being who deserves rest, connection, and a life outside of work.

One of the great myths about running your own practice is that you'll have more freedom. And in some ways, you do—you can set your hours, structure your day, take breaks when you need to. If you're not careful, being your own boss just means your boss is always in the room.

That's why work-life balance and planning for time off are essential for your long-term health, happiness, and sustainability. Without rest, you'll eventually hit burnout. Without boundaries, your practice will swallow your life. And without time to simply *be*, you'll lose touch with the part of you that makes this work so powerful—your heart.

Try to build some work-life balance into your business from the very beginning.

The Emotional Weight of Taking Time Off

Let's start with the emotional stuff because this is often what's hardest to navigate. If you're like many new practitioners, the idea of taking time off may bring up:

Guilt: *"I should be available for my clients."*

Anxiety: *"What if they go to someone else while I'm away?"*

Scarcity: *"I can't afford to miss a week of income."*

Pressure: *"I just need to push through for a little longer..."*

These feelings are completely normal. They come from a place of care—you want to help your clients and grow your business. But they also reflect a mindset that says rest must be earned, or that your value is tied to how available and productive you are.

You do not need to prove your worth by being exhausted.

Rest is not a reward for hard work—it's a requirement for good work.

Planning Your Calendar with Intention

When you're self-employed, no one hands you a leave form. You must create your own system of structure and rest. One of the most helpful things you can do is build out your year in advance—**not just with work goals, but with rest goals too. (**That's what I do. I find if I don't block some time off, it just doesn't happen.)

Here's a practical approach:

Block out your non-negotiables first

Start by deciding how many weeks of proper time off you'd like this year. Even two to three full weeks (not all at once!) can make a difference. Add long weekends, birthday breaks, or mini retreats if that suits you. Mark them in your calendar now.

Add your CPD and admin time

If you need 20+ hours of continuing education each year, don't leave that to the last minute. Block out one or two days per quarter for learning and professional development. Similarly, schedule time for business planning, taxes, marketing, and admin—those tasks don't do themselves.

Notice seasonal patterns

Are you usually quieter in winter? Do clients slow down over the school holidays or Christmas? Use those rhythms to your advantage. That may be the perfect time for a planned break or a reduced schedule.

Communicate your calendar early

Let your regular clients know when you'll be away with plenty of notice. This helps them plan—and reassures them you're not disappearing for good. You can say something like:

"I'll be away from the 10th to the 20th of July, so if you'd like to book around that, let's find a time now."

Being upfront and consistent helps build trust. Most clients respect and appreciate therapists who model self-care.

Income, Time Off, and the Money Worries

Yes, taking time off means time without income. That's real, especially in the early years. But here's where a little planning can go a long way.

You might try:

Saving a percentage of each income cycle in a separate "Time Off" or "Safety Net" account. Even 5–10% can build up faster than you think.

Budgeting your year with gaps in mind, not just month-to-month. Aim to earn enough over ten months to cover twelve and have a back-up plan in place if you don't reach that goal.

Offering packages or prepayments to help smooth out cash flow before a break.

Also, remember—**rest reduces your risk of burnout**. Burnout leads to lost weeks or months of income due to illness, fatigue, or losing your love for the work. Planned rest is an investment, not a luxury.

Daily Rhythms: Balance Isn't Just Holidays

Taking time off doesn't have to mean big blocks. Work-life balance also lives in your **daily and weekly rhythms**.

Ask yourself:

Am I allowing enough time between clients, or am I rushing from one to the next?

Do I stop for lunch, or eat on the go while replying to messages?

Am I checking emails at 10pm?

Do I have a regular day or half-day off that's *off*?

One of the benefits of being your own boss is the flexibility to work in a way that suits your body and your life. If you're a morning person, open early and keep afternoons light. If you have caring responsibilities, shape your hours around them.

Balance doesn't always mean equal—it means *right for you*.

Saying No, Gently and Firmly

Saying no to a client who wants an unreasonably last-minute weekend spot, or to someone who wants to squeeze in during your planned day off, can be confronting. Especially when you care deeply and want to help.

Every time you say yes to something that drains you, you're saying no to the parts of your life that replenish you.

You're not a bad therapist for having boundaries. You're a better one.

Rest as a Form of Professionalism

Rest makes you sharper, more attentive, more emotionally present. Clients can tell when you're centred—and when you're running on fumes. The energy you bring into the room matters. And it's incredibly healing for a client to be cared for by someone who is calm, well, and grounded.

It also models something powerful. When clients see that you take breaks, honour your needs, and return refreshed, it gently invites them to consider doing the same in their own lives. That's part of your ripple effect.

A Personal Reflection

Earlier on, one of my clients fell asleep mid-treatment. I panicked, as I was unsure whether to stop, keep going, or gently wake them up! It reminded me that clients often feel safest when we are centred, calm, and relaxed.

That kind of deep presence isn't something you can feign. It comes from having enough rest, rhythm, and space in your own life to be fully present.

You Deserve a Life, Too

You are more than your bookings. More than your inbox. More than the number of clients you see in a week.

You are a whole person. And your work will thrive—not shrink—when you care for yourself as kindly as you care for others.

Schedule the break. Honour your evenings. Eat the lunch. Take the day off. Set the boundary.

Not just because you've earned it.

But because you *need* it.

Because you *deserve* it.

Because this is your one life—and it's worth living well.

Chapter 32: Avoiding Burnout and Compassion Fatigue

You can love your work deeply—and still become exhausted by it. Awareness is the first step. Boundaries are the second. Recovery is possible.

Massage therapy is often described as a healing profession. But what isn't talked about enough is how much of yourself you pour into your work.

You give with your hands, but also with your heart, your nervous system, your energy. You create safety, connection, and relief for your clients. And many of them walk through your door carrying trauma, grief, exhaustion, or pain. It's a privilege to hold space for them. But it can also be profoundly draining if you're not careful.

Even when you love the work—and especially when you do—there is a risk of burnout and compassion fatigue.

This chapter is a gentle and honest conversation about how to recognise the warning signs early, how to create sustainable rhythms that support your wellbeing, and how to stay connected to the passion that brought you here in the first place—without losing yourself in the process.

The Truth About Burnout

Let's begin by unpacking what burnout *really* is.

Burnout isn't just feeling tired. It's a state of physical, mental, and emotional exhaustion caused by prolonged, unmanaged stress. It doesn't happen overnight. It builds over time—quietly, subtly—until you feel like you're running on fumes.

For massage therapists, burnout often shows up as:

Dreading the workday, even when clients are lovely

Feeling emotionally flat or distant during sessions

Increasing irritability or tearfulness

Trouble concentrating or making decisions

Physical fatigue that sleep doesn't fix

Loss of motivation or joy in your work

A deep desire to escape, quit, or disappear—even if business is going well

If this feels familiar, you're not weak. You're not lazy. You're not failing. You're just human—and your nervous system is waving a white flag.

Understanding Compassion Fatigue

Compassion fatigue is closely linked to burnout but has its own unique signature. It occurs when you've been exposed to others' suffering over a prolonged period—especially without adequate recovery time.

You might notice:

Emotional numbness or feeling disconnected from your clients' stories

Increased cynicism or resentment ("Why does everyone want so much from me?")

A sense of hopelessness or feeling ineffective

Trouble caring about things you usually love

Emotional withdrawal, even from friends and family

Compassion fatigue is particularly common in caring professions—and often misunderstood. Some therapists even feel ashamed to talk about it, fearing it means they've "stopped caring."

Feeling compassion fatigue doesn't mean you don't care—it means you've cared too much, for too long, without enough rest or replenishment.

Why This Work Can Take a Toll

Massage therapy is physically demanding—but also emotionally absorbing.

You listen. You respond. You notice non-verbal cues. You adjust. You bear witness to trauma, chronic illness, loneliness, anxiety, grief. And many of your clients may be used to feeling unsafe or unseen. Your care becomes a sanctuary—and that's a beautiful thing. But it also comes with weight.

If you don't create enough space for your own body, mind, and heart to rest, you will eventually pay the price.

The Early Warning Signs

Burnout and compassion fatigue don't always come with sirens and flashing lights. More often, they creep in through small cracks.

Here are some early signs to watch out for:

You cancel your own appointments (doctor, dentist, massage) because you're "too busy"

You fantasise about quitting or running away

You feel increasingly resentful of clients who are late, demanding, or emotional

You rush through sessions or feel relief when they cancel

You're always "on" but never fully present

You have no time, energy, or desire for hobbies, creativity, or connection

These aren't signs that you're bad at your job. They're signs that your nervous system is overloaded—and that it's time to slow down, reset, and receive.

You Are Allowed to Have Boundaries

One of the biggest contributors to burnout in our field is a lack of boundaries.

Boundaries are not walls to keep people out. They're fences that help keep *you* safe—so you can stay open, present, and engaged without being depleted.

Healthy professional boundaries might include:

Not checking client messages after hours

Leaving adequate time between appointments

Saying "no" to clients who repeatedly overstep or drain you

Referring out when someone's needs are beyond your scope

Protecting your own energy by limiting emotional labour during sessions

It's okay to care deeply about your clients. It's also okay to put your own wellbeing first.

In fact, it's necessary.

Recovery Isn't a One-Time Event

When burnout or compassion fatigue hits, many therapists try to fix it with a weekend off. But recovery isn't just about rest—it's about re-patterning.

Here's what that might look like:

Daily grounding rituals – A short walk, a mindful cup of tea, a quiet moment to breathe between clients.

Regular check-ins – Journaling, supervision, or even just asking yourself: "How am I really feeling right now?"

Touch that nourishes you – Massage, osteopathy, acupuncture—something that lets your own body receive.

Time off that's truly off – No admin. No catch-up. Just rest and pleasure.

Creative outlets – Painting, baking, music, gardening—things that remind you who you are *outside* of being a therapist.

Recovery is not indulgence. It's maintenance. Just like your table, sheets, and oils need care—*so do you*.

If you are working for someone else, be careful that you are not being exploited. Ask yourself if your employer is being unreasonable, underpaying you, or forcing unsafe practices. You may need to find somewhere else to work (somewhere where you'll be treated fairly). If you are ever unsure of fair work conditions, you can contact www.fairwork.gov.au in Australia.

A Personal Story

I still remember my first brush with real burnout. It was the end of a long month. I was fully booked. My business was going well, but I found myself crying in the car between clients—unsure why.

The truth was, I had ignored the subtle signs. I had pushed through sore wrists, missed lunch breaks, responded to late-night texts, and taken on too many "extra" clients because I felt bad saying no.

Eventually, my body and mind said "enough."

That moment became a turning point. I rescheduled clients. I took a few days off. I spoke to a supervisor. And I rewrote how I worked—smarter, slower, softer. I returned not just as a better therapist, but as a more whole human.

Preventing Burnout Starts Now

Even if you feel great right now, this chapter is still for you.

Burnout prevention is most effective when it's proactive—not reactive. Here's where you can start:

Set your work hours and honour them

Keep one admin-only day or half-day a week

Schedule your breaks first when you plan your calendar

Learn to say no with grace

Build peer support into your business (you don't have to do this alone)

Check in with yourself as often as you check in with your clients.

You Are Worth Preserving

This work matters. You matter.

But your wellbeing is not a footnote. It is the foundation. Without it, there is no sustainable career—only a series of crashes and comebacks.

So please, take rest seriously. Protect your energy fiercely. Honour your needs unapologetically.

Let your career be a source of purpose and pride—not a path to exhaustion.

You can still care deeply—and stay well.

You can still give generously—without giving everything.

And you can still love this work—without letting it consume you.

"You cannot serve from an empty vessel." — *Eleanor Brownn*

Chapter 33: Pivoting and Evolving Your Career

"Just because you chose something once doesn't mean you have to choose it forever."

Massage therapy is a dynamic, people-centred profession—but that doesn't mean you'll stay in the same lane forever. Sometimes, what used to light you up begins to dim. Your hands might get tired, your schedule might feel too rigid, or your interests might start to drift into other areas of care.

This chapter is about recognising when it's time for a shift, understanding the options available to you, and approaching change not as failure, but as evolution.

Because change is inevitable.

Listening for the Nudge

The first signs that something isn't quite right in your professional world are rarely dramatic. They're small, persistent nudges:

- A feeling of restlessness, even when things are "going well."

- Not looking forward to your workday, even with great clients.

- Being drawn to courses, conversations, or books outside your current scope.

- Wondering what it might be like to do "something else"—without knowing what that is yet.

These little whispers can be easy to ignore—especially when you've worked so hard to build your business or career. But ignoring them doesn't make them go away. It just delays the inevitable.

Your career is not a cage. It's a living thing. It can stretch. It can shift. It can grow.

Signs It Might Be Time to Pivot

Everyone has off days, but if you've been feeling disconnected for a while, it might be time to explore your next step. Here are some indicators:

- Chronic physical fatigue, pain, or injury that's making hands-on work hard to sustain.

- Emotional exhaustion or burnout that doesn't improve with rest or boundary-setting.

- New interests or passions pulling your attention elsewhere.

- A growing desire to teach, write, lead, or advocate.

- Personal or family changes that make your current workload or hours unworkable.

- A quiet (or loud!) longing for change that won't go away.

- An employer who is making your work life miserable.

None of these mean you've made a mistake. They simply mean you're human—and evolving.

Common Pivot Points in a Massage Career

There are many ways to evolve your massage career without walking away from it completely. Some possibilities include:

Specialising

You might decide to go deeper into an area that lights you up: oncology massage, lymphatic work, sports recovery, pregnancy care, or trauma-informed practice. Specialisation can refresh your enthusiasm and attract a clearer, more aligned client base.

Expanding into Teaching or Mentoring

If you love explaining concepts and supporting other therapists, teaching could be a natural fit. This might be formal (through RTOs or workshops) or informal (mentoring new graduates, creating online courses, writing educational content).

Creating Resources

Writing blogs, workbooks, guides, or books can give voice to your experience and knowledge. This can become a new income stream and deepen your impact beyond the treatment room.

Integrating Complementary Modalities

Many therapists incorporate other healing tools like breathwork, coaching, reflexology, yoga therapy, aromatherapy, or energy work. You don't have to abandon massage—just expand what you offer.

Consulting or Business Coaching

If you've built a successful practice, others may want to learn from you. Business coaching for therapists is an emerging niche with a lot of heart and value.

Changing Formats

You might move from hands-on practice to product-based work, or from full-time hours to a part-time consultancy. There are many ways to shift without exiting completely.

Stepping Away Entirely

And sometimes, the most authentic pivot is to something else entirely. That doesn't erase the value of your work—it adds to the richness of your journey. You're allowed to grow in new directions.

Making the Shift: One Step at a Time

Pivots don't always require a dramatic leap. They can begin with questions:

- What lights me up right now?

- What feels heavy?

- What's missing from my work or life?

- What would I do more of, if I could?

Then come the tiny experiments. You might enrol in a course that excites you. Try training in a new technique and offering a new service. Reduce your clinic hours to make space for something else. Write one blog post. Reach out to a mentor. Shadow someone in a different field.

Think of it as planting seeds. Not all of them will grow—but some might surprise you.

You're Allowed to Change

So many therapists feel guilty or anxious about wanting something different. After all, didn't you choose this path with your whole heart? Didn't you work hard to build it?

Yes. And you're still allowed to want more, or different, or new.

You are not your job title. You are not your modality. You are allowed to evolve. Your identity can hold all the versions of you, past and future.

A Career is Not a Contract

The story of your career is still unfolding. You don't have to have it all figured out. Just keep listening.

Sometimes the most honest, brave thing you can do is say: *"This isn't quite right anymore. I'm ready for something else."*

There is no shame in that. Only honesty. And possibility.

Whether you pivot slightly or change direction entirely, know that your skills, compassion, experience, and care will never be wasted. They will come with you—into whatever comes next.

Chapter 34: Planning for Long-Term Growth

Build a practice that grows with you—not one that outgrows you.

Starting a massage career is exciting, but it's easy to get stuck in survival mode—filling your calendar, chasing client bookings, trying to make ends meet. And while those initial stages *do* require hustle and flexibility, it's equally important to pause and ask yourself a powerful question:

What am I building—and is it sustainable for me?

Long-term growth isn't just about having more clients or making more money (though those things matter too). It's about creating a practice that supports your life—not one that takes over it. It's about building in ways that feel nourishing, not just necessary.

This chapter invites you to zoom out and dream forward.

Growth Doesn't Mean "More of the Same"

Sometimes we assume growth is about *scaling up*—adding more hours, more services, more locations. But growth can also mean:

- Narrowing your niche so you serve fewer clients more deeply
- Shifting from hands-on work to teaching, mentoring, or writing
- Introducing online offerings, workshops, or memberships
- Hiring another therapist or creating a collaborative team
- Reducing hours and raising rates to protect your health
- Setting out on your own if you're currently working for someone

Growth that feels good is growth that's aligned. Before you plan anything, ask yourself:

"What does success look like *for me*—not just what I see other therapists doing?"

Creating a Vision with Room to Evolve

You don't need a five-year plan carved in stone. But you *do* need a direction—a compass.

Try journaling on questions like:

- What kind of work do I want to be doing in 3 years?

- What skills or interests am I curious to develop?

How do I want my work to feel in my body and my life?

What are the warning signs I'm heading toward burnout or boredom?

Your answers might surprise you. Growth doesn't have to look like ambition. It can look like *ease*.

Investing in Yourself

Continued learning is key to long-term sustainability. Whether it's clinical skills, business strategy, or personal development, staying engaged helps you stay inspired.

You might choose to:

- Take CPD courses that light you up (not just tick the box)
- Attend in-person workshops to break routine and network
- Learn new modalities or deepen your expertise in one
- Explore business mentoring, coaching, or peer supervision

Set a learning budget or savings goal just for you. Future You will thank you.

Systems That Can Grow With You

The systems you set up now should be able to stretch as you evolve.

This might mean:

- Choosing booking software that allows for add-on services or multiple team members
- Creating reusable templates for client forms, marketing, and admin
- Documenting your procedures now, so you can one day delegate or outsource
- Starting an email list or basic content library, even if you don't use it much yet

It's easier to build a foundation while things are quiet than when you're already overwhelmed.

Planning Financially for Growth

Growth requires resources. And while you don't need a full financial planner, it helps to:

- Review your income and expenses regularly
- Set aside money for tax, sick leave, holidays, and emergencies
- Have a separate account for continuing education or equipment upgrades
- Plan price increases ahead of time, not in a panic

If you'd like more guidance, we go into financial systems and pricing strategy in earlier chapters—but here's the big takeaway:

Long-term sustainability includes being paid properly. It is more difficult to grow from a place of financial scarcity.

Reviewing and Recalibrating

What works now might not work forever—and that's okay.

270

Set aside time every few months or at the end of each year to review:

- What's working well?

- What's feeling heavy or draining?

- What might you want to shift, simplify, or let go of?

You might find that your goals have changed. That's not failure—it's wisdom.

A Note from the Future

I've worked with so many massage therapists who burn brightly in the beginning... and burn out a few years later.

They didn't fail. They just didn't pause to plan for the long haul.

Let your vision evolve. Let your business grow with you, not against you. Build something that sustains your body, your spirit, and your life outside the clinic walls.

Because this isn't just a career—it's your livelihood, your legacy, and your life.

Chapter 35: Facing Challenges and Setbacks

"Every career has potholes. The trick is learning how to climb out without losing your sense of direction."

If you've ever watched someone on social media who seems to have a perfect clinic, perfect branding, and perfect confidence... pause. You're only seeing a curated moment. Behind every polished website and glowing testimonial is a backstory full of missteps, quiet doubts, slow days, and second guesses.

Challenges and setbacks aren't detours. They *are* the road. In this chapter, we're going to explore some of the common bumps and bruises of massage practice—financial, emotional, physical—and how to respond to them with resilience, self-compassion, and perspective.

You're not alone in this. And you don't have to have it all figured out.

The Early Wobbles Are Normal

Let's normalise a few things:

- Your first few months might be quiet. That doesn't mean you're failing.

- You might question your pricing—even after thinking it through ten times.

- You might have clients cancel last-minute (or worse—just not show up).

- You might find yourself comparing your practice to someone else's.

- You might accidentally double-book someone, forget a client's name, or realise you used the wrong oil for someone with a sensitivity.

These are not signs you're unqualified. They're signs you're human.

No therapist is immune from the awkward starts. They're part of building confidence.

Common Challenges and How to Face Them

Financial Fluctuations

Whether you're working as a sole trader, contractor or employee income can be unpredictable. School holidays, seasonal dips, illness, or just quiet weeks happen.

What helps:

- Having a buffer account or emergency fund, even a small one.

- Tracking your income weekly to see patterns over time.

- Offering value-based promotions (not discounts) during slower periods—like themed packages, gift certificates, or bundled sessions.

- Talking to a bookkeeper or mentor about budgeting for lumpy income.

"One winter, I had two full weeks where only three clients booked in. I panicked. But I also used that time to build a new treatment menu, write blog content, and set up automations. A few weeks later, bookings picked up—and I was more prepared."

Physical Injuries or Fatigue

Repetitive strain injuries (RSI), tendonitis, lower back pain—it happens. We work with our bodies, and that means we need to protect them.

What helps:

- Being honest about your body's limits.

- Investing in ergonomic tools (stools, bolsters, adjustable tables).

- Getting regular bodywork *yourself*—not just giving it.

- Learning technique variations that reduce stress on your joints.

- Considering insurance that covers income loss due to injury.

"I sprained my wrist moving house and couldn't work for two weeks. I had no backup plan. Now I book one admin day a month to review my processes and make sure my health doesn't fall off the list."

Negative Feedback or Complaints

It stings. Even if it's minor. Even if it's unfair. But how you handle it can be a defining moment.

What helps:

- Listening with curiosity, not defensiveness.

- Asking a peer or supervisor to help you debrief.

- Having a complaints policy so you can respond consistently.

- Remembering that one client's opinion does *not* define your worth.

"A client once told me the room was too cold and that I seemed 'distracted'. It hurt. But when I reflected, I realised I was distracted that day. It helped me recommit to staying present—even when life is noisy."

Emotional Exhaustion

Working with people in pain—physically or emotionally—can take its toll.

What helps:

- Supervision or peer support groups.

- Daily or weekly grounding rituals.

- Making sure your calendar includes joy, rest, and movement.

- Recognising when it's time to take a break—or ask for help.

"After a month of clients sharing really heavy stuff, I found myself zoning out mid-session. I debriefed with a colleague, and it was like opening a pressure valve. I needed to say things out loud I didn't realise I was carrying."

Self-Doubt and Comparison

This is a quiet challenge—but a powerful one. You might wonder:

- "Am I good enough?"

- "Why isn't my practice as busy as theirs?"

- "Maybe I'm not cut out for this..."

What helps:

- Journaling your wins, big or small.

- Unsubscribing from social media accounts that leave you feeling inadequate.

- Surrounding yourself with peers who are honest—not just glossy.

- Remembering: the only comparison that matters is you, yesterday to today.

Reframing "Failure"

Setbacks can feel personal, but more often than not, they're just part of the natural rhythm of growth.

- The no-show taught you to tighten your policies.

- The client complaint taught you to communicate more clearly.

- The quiet month reminded you to revisit your marketing.

- The burnout taught you to rest before you're depleted.

Failure is information. It teaches. It redirects. It shapes us.

You Don't Have to Pretend It's All Fine

You Are A Work In Progress

The road ahead will present more challenges and opportunities.

Your value isn't in perfection—it's in how imperfection shapes you as an individual who is increasingly resilient, seasoned, and grounded.

You are the real deal.

And You, and your career, will grow.

Chapter 36: Continuing Education and Lifelong Learning

"You're not finished—you're just getting started."

Graduating with your massage qualification feels like the finish line—and in many ways, it is. But it's also the *starting line* for something else: your ongoing development as a practitioner.

Whether you're required to complete a certain number of Continuing Professional Education (CPE or CPD) hours each year, or you're simply passionate about doing your work better, lifelong learning is a cornerstone of a sustainable and satisfying career, and life in general.

This chapter is about more than just ticking the boxes. It's about growing your skills, your confidence, your creativity, and your capacity to care.

Let's explore how to make ongoing learning feel exciting—not overwhelming—and how to choose education that supports the kind of therapist (and human) you want to be.

Why Lifelong Learning Matters

You don't need to know everything at once. But the more you learn, the more flexible, confident, and supported you'll feel in your practice.

Lifelong learning helps you:

- Stay up to date with evidence-informed practices and safety guidelines
- Deepen your knowledge in areas you're passionate about
- Discover new interests and modalities
- Avoid stagnation and burnout
- Expand your career options
- Meet your professional obligations for association or provider status
- Stay connected with the wider professional community

"The more I learn, the more I realise how much more there is to explore. And that's exciting, not intimidating. It means I get to keep growing."

What Counts as Continuing Education?

Depending on your association and location, continuing education might include:

- Short courses (in-person or online)

- Accredited certificate programs

- Attending conferences or symposiums

- Reading academic journals or relevant publications

- Peer discussions or clinical supervision

- Completing business-related training

- Attending safety or first aid updates

- Teaching or presenting (in some cases)

Always check the specific CPE/CPD policy of your professional association, as requirements vary.

Choosing Education That Aligns With Your Practice

There are so many options out there. So how do you choose?

Ask yourself:

- What skills or techniques would help me better serve my current clients?

- What areas genuinely excite me or spark curiosity?

- What gaps do I feel in my confidence or knowledge?

- Am I interested in growing my clinical skills, my business systems, or both?

- What kinds of clients do I want to attract more of—and what education might support that?

"I started out wanting to learn about lymphatic drainage because I had one client who'd had surgery. It turned into a whole new pathway I didn't expect—but absolutely love."

You don't have to follow the latest trend. Choose what feels meaningful and useful to *you*.

Making Learning Sustainable

You don't have to overload yourself. Some therapists complete their CPE all at once, while others sprinkle it across the year. Find a rhythm that works with your life and budget.

Tips:

- Set a yearly education budget (even a small one).

- Track what you've completed and what you want to learn next.

- Try one "stretch" topic and one "comfort zone" topic each year.

- Consider a mix of formal and informal learning.

- Learn with a friend or colleague to stay motivated.

Learning doesn't always mean a course. Whether you're reading this book, attending a webinar, or reflecting on client cases with peers, it all counts as continued professional learning.

Reframing Professional Development

Let's be honest—CPE can feel like a chore when we're tired, busy, or unsure what to choose. But what if we reframed it as a gift?

Continuing education is a chance to:

- Reignite your passion

- Reconnect with your purpose

- Reclaim a sense of curiosity

- Renew your skills

- Reimagine your practice

- Meet other like-minded professionals

You don't need to become a walking encyclopedia. You just need to keep asking: *what would help me grow right now?*

You're Allowed to Evolve

You don't have to be (you won't be) the same therapist you were last year, or last month for that matter

Your learning path will reflect your life, your clients, your values, and your dreams.

It's a good thing.

Whether you're diving into a big certification, picking up a book on trauma awareness, learning new tech skills to streamline your bookings, or joining a peer supervision group—know this:

Every time you learn, you're investing in yourself.
Every time you grow, your clients benefit too.
And every time you say yes to learning, you're saying yes to a future

that feels richer, steadier, and more aligned with who you're becoming.

Professional Development Planning Worksheet

Your Name: _____

Year: _____

1. Reflecting on Where You Are Now

Take a few minutes to jot down your thoughts.

What parts of your work do you feel most confident in?

_____

_____

What situations or client presentations make you feel unsure?

_____

_____

What topics are you curious to explore further?

_____

_____

What's one area of practice you'd like to feel stronger in?

_____

_____

2. Setting Your Learning Goals

Think about your next steps—big or small.

Learning Goal	Why It Matters to Me	How I'll Learn (Course, Book, Peer Group etc.)	When?

3. Beyond the Textbooks

Growth isn't just formal learning. Let's broaden it.

A professional I'd love to learn from:

A book or podcast I want to explore:

A topic I'd enjoy discussing with peers:

A way I can stretch myself this year:

A small "win" I want to celebrate by the end of the year:

4. Accountability & Reflection

Who will I check in with about my learning goals?

When will I revisit this plan?

Yearly CPE Tracker Template

Name:

Membership/Association:

CPE Hours Required:

Year:

Date	Activity	Provider	Hours Earned	Notes/Reflections

Total Hours Completed: _____

Comments or thoughts about this year's learning experience:

Chapter 37: Making It Sustainable – Turning Passion into a Real Living

When I first started out, I kept wondering if this was going to work. I loved what I did—but love doesn't pay the bills. I'd look at my calendar and see more blank space than bookings, and I'd second-guess everything: my prices, my skills, even the decision to go into massage in the first place.

Sound familiar?

This chapter is here to reassure you: **you absolutely can make massage a viable, sustainable career.** But it takes some planning, a willingness to adapt, and a mindset that blends *care* with *strategy*.

Let's talk honestly about what it really looks like.

Pricing for Sustainability

It's tempting to set low prices when you're starting out—because you want clients, because you're not sure of your worth yet, or because you're comparing yourself to everyone else. But here's the truth:

If your pricing doesn't support your living expenses, your self-care, and your professional growth, it's not sustainable.

Start by working backwards:

What are your monthly expenses (business + personal)?

How many hours a week do you *want* to work?

What price point supports that?

There's no one-size-fits-all number. But it needs to *work for you*. If you're undercharging out of fear or self-doubt, it will eventually lead to burnout—or resignation.

Income Planning: Feast or Famine

Massage income can be unpredictable, especially at first. You might have weeks that are fully booked, followed by slow patches that knock your confidence.

To plan for this:

- Set up a separate business bank account
- Create a buffer (even a few hundred dollars helps)
- Don't rely on last-minute bookings—build routines with re-bookings
- Know your "bare minimum" income target each month
- Track what works—and don't panic during the slow weeks

Multiple Income Streams

The one thing I hear from massage therapists repeatedly is whether they should diversify their income or business by selling oils or other products.

It's Not About Adding *More*—It's About Doing It *Well With What You Already Have And Know*

A sustainable massage business isn't built on working all hours, undercharging, or scrambling for every client. It's built on:

- Knowing your worth
- Pricing to sustain your life and business
- Building relationships that last
- Creating habits that support you

This is possible. You don't need to sell products on the side or teach classes to make ends meet if you don't want to. **You can build a career focused on massage alone—if you build it thoughtfully.**

Work Smarter, Not Just Harder

You don't have to be booked solid 40 hours a week to make a living. In fact, please don't be. That's a shortcut to burnout.

Instead:

- Charge rates that reflect your value

- Create rebooking systems so your clients return consistently

- Automate what you can (reminders, bookings, follow-ups)

- Protect your time—use policies, breaks, and boundaries

Think in Seasons, Not Weeks

Sustainability is about rhythm. There might be months that are slower—and that's not failure. It's normal. Use the quiet times to review your business, update your website, plan promotions, or just *rest*.

Trust that things build over time. One happy client leads to three more. One quiet month might be followed by two chaotic ones.

You don't have to do it all today. You just have to **keep showing up with care and clarity.**

Reflection

Write down your sustainability statement:

"My business will feel sustainable and make me happy when I _____."

(e.g., see ten clients a week, take two days off, earn $X/month, take school holidays off, have time to actually enjoy my life, etc.)

Come back to this as a check-in. It's not just about surviving. It's about building a working life that feels good, too.

You Won't Always Feel Ready—But You're Capable

You made it to the final chapter—and that means something. Not just that you've read the book, but that you've *committed* to this leap into your massage career with heart, courage, and curiosity.

There's no certificate waiting for you here. No test to prove you've memorised every step. Because the truth is, your real learning will happen out there—in the quiet hum of your clinic, the unexpected conversations with clients, the moments you doubt yourself and choose to keep going anyway.

This book was never about telling you *exactly* what to do. It was about giving you enough information, enough reassurance, and enough direction to help you build something that feels like yours.

No one has all the answers at the beginning. Most of us are still figuring things out, years in. The good news? You don't need to be perfect. You just need to be present, thoughtful, and open to learning.

You'll grow into your confidence, one booking at a time.

You'll get better at saying no, setting boundaries, adjusting your prices, navigating the occasional awkward moment.

You'll learn what lights you up—and what doesn't.

You'll try things that don't work, and that's okay. It's not failure—it's information.

You Deserve Support

Running a massage practice—or working in one—is often a solitary path. But it doesn't have to be isolating.

Be available to connect with peers. Reach out for supervision. Celebrate the wins and unpack the tough days with people who get it.

And if you ever feel stuck or unsure, you can come back to this book. Or to your notes. Or to the version of yourself who decided to take this leap in the first place.

She or he or they knew you were capable—even if you forget sometimes.

Your Practice Will Evolve. So Will You.

You don't have to have it all figured out. Your vision may shift. Your niche might narrow or expand. You might pivot into teaching, lymphatic work, oncology massage, business mentoring, or something you haven't even imagined yet.

There's no "one right way" to be a massage therapist.

There's just *your* way—and permission to keep refining it as you grow.

Thank You for Letting Me Be Part of This

Writing this book has been a labour of love—because I remember what it felt like to start. I remember wondering how much to charge, worrying whether I was good enough, wondering if anyone would book in again.

And I remember the first time a client fell asleep on my table... and I wasn't sure if that was a good thing or a bad thing!

If any part of this book has made you feel seen, less alone, or more prepared—you've made my day. Truly.

What's Next?

Maybe now you're ready to set up your room, build your booking system, design your website, or have a quiet cry from relief that you're not the only one feeling overwhelmed (you're not).

Maybe now is the time to rest. Or plan. Or print that vision board worksheet.

Perhaps you'll explore one of our other resources or courses, especially if there's a topic you'd like to dive deeper into. Choose what feels helpful right now and come back to the rest later. You don't have to do it all at once.

Whatever comes next, I'm cheering for you.

Take the leap.

You've already begun.

Explore More In-Depth Learning

If you loved this book and want to go deeper into specific areas, check out our other books and courses:

- **Create A Niche and Stand Out in A Crowd** – Not just a list of services. Discover who you really want to help.

- **Imposter Syndrome: From Self-Doubt to Confidence** – A course designed especially for massage therapists who wonder if they're "enough." (You are.)

- **Case Studies in Remedial Massage Therapy** – Learn how to write, analyse, and use case studies in real-world practice—without needing a research degree.

- **The Quiet Unravelling** – Understand and recover from burnout and compassion fatigue, with companion resources for both therapists and humans.

All courses include worksheets, videos, and loads of extra resources.

Browse at www.massagecpe.com.au

www.ingramcontent.com/pod-product-compliance
Lightning Source LLC
Chambersburg PA
CBHW080356030426
42334CB00024B/2892